AVIVA REIMER

Becoming

THE TOTAL PACKAGE

Choose The Love You Deserve
For the Life You Want

Foreword by Dr. Jila Yazhary

Becoming The Total Package
By Aviva Reimer

ISBN 978-10730762-7-7

Printed in Canada

https://www.avivareimer.com

Table of Contents

Dedication

This book is dedicated to Linda Hamori, my soul sister and best friend for over 25 years. A true friend who shares her heart, never judges, always understands, and has been my supportive rock no matter what life presents us with. We've lost, we've gained, we've cried, we've laughed, we've learned, and have always "chosen" to succeed. I will love you and appreciate you always as we grow old together in our friendship and adventure. You are a gift!

Foreword

Having read *Becoming The total Package* in its original transcript form, I applaud Aviva's work. She has not only incorporated what I, as a counselor, have provided my patients, but taken many of those psychological concepts and added a further and more effective venue. With her innovation, Aviva has created a movement in this present social setting that I can only observe and admire.

I am proud of Aviva and support and appreciate her excellent book. May *Becoming The Total Package* rejuvenate and inspire many people to reach their potential and relate to others with grace and joy.

- Dr. Jila Yazhary, Psychotherapist,
MSc Psychology, MSc Counseling

Introduction

Before we begin, you should know a few things up front. This book is about renovating your life and creating the possibility of everything you feel you want and deserve. In short, it's about becoming the Total Package. Even though I might be a relationship expert and matchmaker, this book isn't just geared for people wanting relationships. It's for everyone who wants to protect their self-worth, build confidence, become more self aware, start a new chapter, and create a more rewarding life. This isn't about *finding* the right partner, but *becoming* the right partner for the person you desire the most. Become the most desirable version of yourself, and you don't need to go looking for your ideal partner, he or she will find you.

The future is built every day and it all starts with you!

This isn't about becoming someone else. Your "best self" is still you, and it's up to you to discover what that looks like. The greatest version of you doesn't have to look like me, some TV celebrity, or anyone else other than you. Nor does all of this focus on change and transformation mean that you are somehow unworthy of love and abundance as you are (as we'll learn in the first chapter, that is a limiting belief, and completely untrue). You are worthy of love and abundance simply by virtue of the fact that you are a human being.

This book is for people who are in a not-so-great place or in a funk, going through relationship breakdowns, depression, low self-esteem, loss of friendships, jobs, and other heartbreaks. It's also for people who aren't doing so badly, but who want to take their lives to the next level. I help people structure their lives so they end up with the most they can possibly have and be. And it's never too late!

The Universe works holistically. Your physical health, your living space, your job, and your relationships (both intimate and non-romantic) all have parts to play in helping you create a life that you love. We'll explore how getting all those aspects of your life together will, among all of the other amazing achievements that you will have, help you attract a romance for the ages.

We'll explore how to approach the traditional avenues of meeting people – in person, online dating, and matchmaking services – but only after you have done the work of getting yourself and your life into a state of high vibration, good health, excellent presentation, and deep self-awareness.

Don't we all have those persistent, predictable issues that seem to crop up sooner or later in life? They're related to beliefs that you've held since your early years that cause you, subconsciously, to say certain things or take specific actions that damage or destroy your relationships and self-worth. I'll show you how to uncover what those beliefs are and provide you with clear guidance on how to heal them.

If, up until this point, you've been unable to find a love that lasts, don't worry. There are barriers, some hidden, some obvious to everyone else, that are keeping you from experiencing it. We'll break through them together. And if you're not in a relationship, or if there are other aspects of your life where you're unhappy, you'll also have the tools to be able to optimize your life to be the way you want it to be.

I will show you step by step how to choose wisely. It's about retraining your mind to get into certain healthy routines and establishing a stronger emotional and physical foundation, which will then spill over into other aspects of your life and create confidence and happiness. This is a restructuring of your previous conditioning, the kind of conditioning that came from negative experiences and limiting beliefs.

No matter what you're going through, no matter what happens with anyone else, you will have your own strong armor that nothing and no one can penetrate. No matter how bad it gets, you will always be okay. Everyone can develop their own armor: I've found mine. The key to this is taking control and making the changes necessary to create a happy life based on integrity, logic, and substance. By doing so, you'll build an authentic confidence, the kind that's so strong within you that no matter how challenging things seem to get, you'll be able to stay in control of yourself, and the rest of your life.

Our minds, our environment, and the people we surround ourselves with all have a significant impact on our lives and the decisions that we make. We are going to look at every aspect of your life, your thoughts, your home, your health, your self -image, and your relationships.

Who This Book is For

This book is for those who have suffered too many heartbreaks and disappointments but still can't figure out just why they keep happening. This is for people who are ready to take responsibility for themselves and their lives in a way that isn't about self-blame or self-hatred, but about taking back your power from false ideas, people in your life who have kept you disempowered, and past experiences that continue to haunt you.

Most of all, it's for people who are willing to do the work on themselves. The solutions I offer here may be simple, but they are certainly not easy to undertake. Remember: transformation is holistic, and involves every major part of your life. Through this book, I will help you craft your own action plans to carry out these exercises, as well as back-up plans for when (not if) you slip up.

What will these exercises involve?

- You'll finally (and literally) put your house in order so that your space will be happy, bright, and conducive to helping you feel relaxed and clear minded. Every time you walk in the door, you will feel safe and comfortable.
- You'll get yourself into the best physical shape you've ever been in, the best of your entire life! You'll look and feel incredibly re-energized and confident.
- You will resolve long-standing issues from your past that continue to sabotage aspects of your life today, by listing them out using a time-tested process that delivers proven results.

- You will re-evaluate your closest friendships and relationships, ensuring that you are surrounding yourself only with the people who lift you up, believe in, and support you!
- You will establish your new boundaries in all your relationships, in order to build respect with others.
- All of those little projects that have held you back or that take up room in the back of your mind? You'll finally complete them with integrity.
- You will learn how to let go of things that clutter your mind and space.
- I will show you how to revamp your wardrobe to suit your personality and character.
- Finally, by being your fabulous self, you'll be in a position to attract the relationship of your dreams.

In short, you will become the Total Package, both for yourself and everyone around you!

Together, in the chapters ahead, I will guide you with a realistic and logical perspective through every aspect of your life, so you can start making new decisions that will allow you to grow and create the best version of yourself and the life you want.

Remember: it is a choice.

Happiness is a Choice

Did you know that happiness is a choice? It's true.

What is love today? Love is one of the most incredible feelings that you will experience in a lifetime.

So, what does that mean in today's world? What does that mean for the generations to come? More and more, love is becoming harder to find and maintain. Lack of trust is being instilled in people instead of faith. Who will teach the younger generations how to appreciate the meaning of true love? Who will teach them what love is supposed to look like? How it's supposed to be perceived and what it is supposed to feel like? Things are challenging in today's world of dating and love, no matter what age or gender. Technology is replacing human interaction, and we will soon become robotic without the beauty of a real connection.

Well, I have the answer! Happiness is a choice, and we all have the power to make the right choice in our personal lives. And although the world is changing around us, we can create our own world of change without being swallowed up by the epidemic of negative change around us. You have the power and control of you! It all starts with a thought and a vision, followed by a leap of faith, and the decision to choose differently. Each person must self-reflect to understand oneself and believe in oneself.

Once you take control of your life, anything is possible. It all starts with the mindset that we have a choice. We can choose to think negatively, or we can choose to smile and be happy, realize what is important, and stand by that with integrity and logic. Once you decide, it becomes a lot easier, and great things start to happen. I call that "planting the seed."

You can choose to be the same way in love. Choose to stay connected, decide to be vulnerable, decide to have faith in people. Hold onto chivalry, believe in traditions your grandparents taught you. Create your own path to happiness! It all starts here.

A Tantalizing Possibility

Finally, if you start wondering where all of this is going, I want you to remember this…

Take a moment, right now, and imagine waking up out of a long, long sleep, restless and full of bad dreams. You open your eyes, and for a few seconds, you don't realize that you're awake. You think that you are still living the life of your bad dreams, one filled with disappointments, great sadness, and anxiety.

You sit up in your bed and rub your eyes, the afterglow of the dream still lingering in your head. As you reflect on the dream, you realize that now something is different. You thought that way of life was perfectly normal. You had to be limited, to stay the way that you were, and keep to your routine, no matter how dreary or dreadful.

Now you reach for your glasses, and as you put them on, the realization hits you! You are waking up to your real life. And your real life, your new life, is so much more vibrant than you could have known!

You smile, stepping out of bed and heading over to the window. You pull back the curtains to reveal golden sunlight, and a warm summer morning, fresh and clean as if the world was new. You acknowledge the work you have done, and you feel safe and untouchable in your new, confident armor.

By now, you have the sexy body you've always wanted, and you're having a ball with your new look and wardrobe. You have created a fresh, new home space that is bright and sunny that will de-stress you every time you open the door. You have the support of incredible, positive people that you have chosen to have in your life. And you realize these right decisions have brought you here to your new life and self-awareness, and that *you* made it happen! You look and feel like you are on top of the world. Safe. Untouchable.

Here's something you might not have thought of, everyone wants to be affected by someone who has the positive energy that you now have. People will feel your energy and will naturally gravitate to you.

And one of these people will be the partner of your dreams.

Like attracts like, so put on your seatbelt and get ready for the ride you deserve! This is a possibility that awaits you if you follow the steps in this book. Things are actually starting to transform in your life simply because you have been making the right decisions and choosing *you*. By gradual degrees, you'll notice things changing for the better around you, until one day, you are living your new life.

Becoming the Total Package is not an overnight experience. It'll be baby steps, but it's definitely going to happen. The writing will be on the wall for you, and I'll be there with you, helping you wake up out of your gloomy, present-day dream into that bright, beautiful reality.

Chapter 1

THE NATURE OF THE WORLD & WHAT WE DON'T REALIZE

"In order to know where you are going ... You must understand where you came from."

F irst things first!
Before we get into it, it is essential for me to explain the relevance of what I am about to share with you in these first few pages. I am all about structure when it comes to guiding you, and I believe that before we can clearly understand where we are going in our lives, we must first know where we've come from. To start out, I will lay out how our world truly is (the good, bad and ugly) and how this crazy place affects us. Then it will be your choice to decide whether you wish to live as you have been, or to change your life to exist within the world.

Before we start creating positive change together, we also must think about what kind of impact we want to make on the world. What kind of person do you want to be, and how do you wish to be treated by others?

Here are some perspectives that you should acknowledge and keep in your thoughts, because the changes we are going to make through this book all have relevance to these following few facts:

You are in control of your own destiny.
Everything happens for a reason.
Anything is possible.

When I say you are in control of your destiny, I mean that we all make decisions, and these decisions will take us on a certain path. That path goes into a direction, just like coming to a T in a road and deciding to go left or right. In the same way, you make decisions. Wrong decisions will send you in a negative direction. Right choices will send you in a positive direction. And of course, this is why it's essential to learn from bad decisions, so we don't make them again.

When I say "everything happens for a reason", I mean that our Universe and lives will, at times, dictate what happens without our control. However, it's what we decide to do with those circumstances that matters. The more we grow, the more intuitive we can become, and the more open we become to being able to listen to the Universe and identifying the signs to follow our path. We also learn to not take things so personally so as to try to control them: death, breakups, job losses, etc. All you have to figure out is whether you are willing to look at the Universe with the cup half-empty, or half-full. This is another decision that you need to make that will impact your life.

When I say anything is possible, it truly is! We just need to make you a believer first. The life that we live is like a book, full of chapters and stories of our journey, relationships, and experiences, good and bad. Your right decisions will attract and lead you on a path of positive outcomes, and the Law of Attraction will present itself before your eyes once you start executing the structure laid out in this book. In order to be successful in anything that we do in life, first you must have your vision, then, to solidify that vision you need integrity, positivity, and commitment. It all starts with your vision, however, and that means accepting the possibility, whereas before you might not have.

It all starts with you. Relationships are also about the other person - you have to compromise and put that person first at times - but you also have to love yourself more than anyone else. This is another conscious declaration, and a decision that you will need to make.

Sometimes you can get into a negative headspace. Having a healthy mind and thought process is so necessary that it'll optimize every aspect of your life. People simply don't think outside of this particular box. They have little understanding of how things really work when it comes to love, sex, romance, connection, communication, and other aspects so essential to a healthy relationship. And so they can't grasp the possibilities that are readily available to them.

On a more fundamental level, though, many people don't understand how they always seem to run into the same problems over and over again from one relationship to the next, why they can't seem to get themselves out of some physical rut or emotional funk.

I want you to keep the following close to your thoughts, because later on, when you're making big decisions, it will be relevant to you within your own world.

What if I told you that when you see the world, it's really not as it appears?

Every day, you live your life as if your own personal world is *the* world - that your job, your relationships, your family, your friends, your problems, the city you live in, your favorite shows and hang-out spots are as big as the planet itself. The world is yours.

Of course, it's not true. Your world only seems so significant or meaningful because you're in it. To everyone else, in the grand scheme of life, your world is a grain of sand. The higher, objective world is so much bigger than you and your life.

This isn't how society teaches us to be, though, is it? In our society – and I mean Western, North American society – we say that there's nothing more important than the individual. We put ourselves first – our needs, our beliefs and opinions, our wants – and although (as we'll explore in these pages together) it's definitely important to work on ourselves, it's important to remember that it's not only about us. If we can try to open our eyes and get outside of our own little box that we live in, that consumes all of our attention and energies, and compare ourselves to others, we see that we are not as important in the grand scheme of things, and that's okay.

This is the first part of the true nature of the world. Your issues and challenges may seem like the most significant thing, but they're not, and the only way to see it is to look to other people. It's never just about you.

But that's not where we tend to start.

Everyone in Their Own Box

Imagine yourself as a planet. Everywhere you look, you see the Universe – the stars, the Sun, other worlds – apparently turning around you. Without knowing any better, you'd assume that you are the center of everything, that those stars, the Sun, and planets are all there for you.

In reality, of course, those other bodies up in the sky couldn't be more indifferent to you, but you don't know that right away. You assume that they have some kind of vested interest in everything that's happening in your world.

Here's the kicker though. If you were to go to any of those other planets, you'd find that they think the same thing about you! They assume that you revolved around them! Neither of those things is true. This is your life, right? But everybody's feeling the same way. Everybody thinks they're the most important person in the world, that their problems are the most awful, that everyone should care about their dreams and goals and wins.

This is important to understand when it comes to relationships and life. When you meet new people, what you're doing is meeting someone else who is in their own little box-universe of experience.

When they meet you, they're doing the same thing. Within each of those boxes are different rules, different expectations, different beliefs, different assumptions, and all of them feel like the truth when they are, in fact, only *your* truth and *their* truth. Relationships exist somewhere in the middle.

Most people simply don't realize that they're in their own little box. If I were to wave a magic wand that would take you out of your own small universe and then show yourself to you, as if you were watching yourself in a movie of your own life, like Jim Carrey in *The Truman Show*, you'd have a completely different perspective. You'd see that some of your beliefs simply aren't true. You'd probably want to make some changes to yourself, your belief system, your habits, and your self-image. Every part of your life would be up for grabs if you could see it from the outside looking in. How we perceive ourselves is quite different from how others perceive us.

Here is an excellent example of how we tend to see our self-image. I once heard of someone who hired a forensic artist to perform an experiment. The artist was to sketch a portrait of an individual who sat behind a partition where they could not be seen, and gave verbal description of themselves for the artist to sketch, similar to how an eyewitness would describe a crime suspect. Part Two of that experiment involved having friends of the individual give the artist their descriptions of the same person. Guess what? The two portraits could not be more different. The one that the artist drew based on the friends' descriptions was much more beautiful and vibrant in comparison to the subject's own description of themselves.

The experiment demonstrated the difference of perception. We don't see ourselves the way others do. We may be, and probably are, more beautiful than we believe ourselves to be.

Part of what I want to accomplish in this book is to show you that different point of view around your relationships and self-image. It isn't just about the clothes, the meet-cutes, the horoscopes, and compatibility ratios on OkCupid. It's not about the other person. 90% of what will determine your own success or failure in life (such as dating, relationships, work, etc.) starts with your own self-awareness. It begins by changing your own world and your own perspective.

What You Can('t) Control

Let's talk about control. We're in a personal growth culture that tells people that they can change their circumstances ("change your thoughts, change your life", as the famous mantra from the late, great Wayne Dyer goes, is just one example of it). As a coach and fitness trainer, I absolutely am happy that this is the case. Millions of people now have resources and mentors at their fingertips to help them transform the parts of their lives that they don't want, from basic health and fitness, careers and money, the state of their politics and government, and (of course), their love lives.

Still, what we don't talk about often enough is what we cannot control out of life, and this has consequences for everything around us including any work that we choose to do on ourselves. Let me explain.

You do, in fact, have control. Control over the decisions of your own life and to lead it in any direction that you want. No matter what the world is doing, what the government is doing, regardless of what your next-door neighbor is doing, you can decide things for yourself that have nothing to do with any of them. If there's a lot of negativity happening right now around you, in the news (which there usually is), or at your workplace, you can choose not to be a part of it. You don't have to join that party.

At that point, you can focus your attention on your own world, your own box-universe, develop routines and practices (like exercise, eating well, meditation, or what have you) and optimize your life to ensure that none of that outside negativity can seep into your space. You can create your life in such a way that when you reach the end of it, you can look back and say, "Wow! What a great ride!"

Or, you can accept the invitation to that negativity party and just join in on all of the gossip, the stress, the mess, the anger, and the silence. You can choose to simply look at the crap of the world and say, "everything sucks, this is awful, I'm no good."

Personally, I'd choose the former.

That's really what it's about, isn't it? Those questions at the end of life. Did I make an impact? Did I enjoy things? Did I have fun? Was I happy? Was I miserable? What kind of relationships did I have, what kind of legacy am I leaving (and not just financially, but emotionally and spiritually)? Can I say that I did all the things I wanted, and that I enjoyed my life? Because at the end of the day, we're all gonna go. My favorite saying is, "life is not a dress rehearsal, you have one go of it", so you better choose to make the best of it.

You have only a certain amount of time on the planet and only a certain degree of control over how you spend it.

But you don't have full control.

There are simply some things about which no amount of meditating, willpower, or healthy-eating can change. Disease, war, natural disasters, political upheaval, or even a simple rainstorm on the same day as your family reunion picnic. Forces of nature, the greater forces of society, and the decisions that other human beings make for themselves are, for the most part, out of your control.

The first verse of the Serenity Prayer illustrates the nature of control nicely (and it's good to keep this in your back pocket for those stressful moments and people that you can not change):

God grant me the serenity
to accept the things I cannot change;
the courage to change the things I can;
and the wisdom to know the difference.

Although I am not myself religious (and you may not be either), I find strength and comfort in the verse of Psalm 23,

The Psalm of David, and would like to share this with you for the challenging days that we all experience:

> The Lord is my shepherd; I shall not want.
> He makes me lie down in green pastures.
> He leads me beside still waters.
> He restores my soul.
> He leads me in paths of righteousness
> for his name's sake.
> Even though I walk through the valley of the shadow of
> death,
> I will fear no evil,
> for you are with me;
> your rod and your staff,
> they comfort me.
> You prepare a table before me
> in the presence of my enemies;
> you anoint my head with oil;
> my cup overflows.
> Surely goodness and mercy shall follow me
> all the days of my life,
> and I shall dwell in the house of the Lord
> forever.

And how can you know what the difference is? How can you find the courage to walk in dark places and fear no evil? It starts by knowing yourself.

Life is All About Relationships and Experiences (How does this Affect Each and Every One of Us?)

What does any of this have to do with dating and relationships? Think of it this way. I'll talk to people who've just been through a terrible relationship, and they're down in the dumps. I'll say to them, "you know, there are people all around you, on the other side of the world and right next door, who are going through worse. Someone in a war-torn village in the Congo or Central America is having a limb chopped off by a soldier. Someone, somewhere, in this very city is getting a cancer diagnosis from their doctor. Many people, right now, are on their deathbeds, with no one there to see them."

Often, I'll take their hands in mine before continuing. "I understand that your pain seems like the worst thing in the world right now, and it's understandable. You've just been through an awful hurt, and it's only natural to feel what you feel. But for a moment, I want you to compare your pain to someone else's pain right now, to those people I just mentioned." Usually, they'll be quiet for a few seconds while they imagine those other people. Then I'll ask them. "How do you feel now?"

Of course, they're still going to feel their pain. The point of the exercise isn't to eliminate pain. Pain is part of love, part of life. You need to welcome pain as part of life and growth, as it is inevitable to avoid. But when they put their pain into the context of things happening in the greater world, their pain becomes a little less. They shift their focus from their own pain to compassion for the suffering of others who, at that very moment, are going through worse. For those few seconds of reflection, they've left their own worlds and entered the far more painful experiences of others, only to return and find their own problems not as bad.

There are problems all over the world, just everywhere. You've got your own share of issues and challenges on your plate, and you've got to handle them. I'm not suggesting that you should ignore them, and I'm not trying to diminish what you're going through just because "someone has it worse." This isn't about that, it's simply about giving you perspective on what you've got to go through. It may seem like the biggest problem in the world, which can sometimes rob you of your own sense of power to deal with it. It can be overwhelming and damaging to your physical and mental health. However, by stepping out of your world and into someone else's, you can put that problem into the proper context and see that it is manageable. You are not helpless, and you are not alone.

How you choose to look at your own problems, and what you choose to do with your issues or circumstances when they arise, is in your hands. Each and every human being is moulded differently. How they were raised and the experiences they lived through, good or bad, will differentiate their character, their expectations, reactions, and assumptions in all aspects of life. Now, is it up to us as individuals to rifle through all that and figure them out? When someone does something, there is always a reaction on the receiving end. These reactions can get us in to trouble at times. Perspective is key. That's why it's crucial to learn and choose to have control of our mind and thought process in what we do, as it will always affect our lives. It's a car you can drive, and while you're driving, you're free to turn left, turn right, stop, reverse, or keep going straight ahead. You can pick your direction, and for myself, I know I'd rather go right towards happiness and gratitude. I'd rather drive in the direction of change and transformation instead of going the other way, towards some other place I don't want to be. I tell this to my clients and then say "it's a choice that you have to make."

The vast majority of the time, stepping into someone else's world of experience helps get the healing process off to a running start, and before long, they're ready to look for love again (or just be happy in their own skin, happy with their circumstances in life).

An understanding of how the world actually works – how you perceive others, how others perceive you, what you can control, what you can't – helps you approach your relationships more effectively. The man or woman of your dreams is out there, but as with many things in life, you find what you desire by not looking for it. Instead, you attract the person of your desires by becoming the man or women of their dreams, just by being your best self.

Early Life Lessons

If you think I don't have my shit to deal with, you'd be sorely mistaken. The life that I've led, I had more than a few bumps and bruises on my subconscious.

What I've just shared with you was hard-won knowledge. It comes from several experiences in life. I have been cheated on, I was emotionally abused, my heart was broken many times. I grew up without a lot of attention from my parents. I've had to move across the world. I've had to do all of this work just to survive. Because I've experienced all of these things, they have conditioned me to be a survivor. In my experiences and therapy that I've come to have through my life lessons, I'm now able to share the recipe with you. Experiences in my own transformation at an early age of my life have given me the ability to help everyone now. Low self-worth and limiting beliefs. I rebelled, hung out with the wrong kids, skipped school, tried smoking, drinking, partying, coming home late.

No one is born with a clear perspective on how things really work, but for as long as I can remember, the one thing I can say for sure is that I am, and always have been, someone who wanted to help people.

I've experienced a little bit of the good, quite a bit of the bad, and even some of the ugly. I had to make many hard choices for myself. Though many of these experiences were very different from each other, when I look back, I see that the one common thread in how they all turned out was a single question: "what kind of person do I want to be?"

It's a simple question, sure, but it's often led me to some very hard choices. "Simple" doesn't always mean "easy." In fact, some of the right decisions are not always easy to make.

Who do I want to be? Do I want to be somebody who's always affected by negative things and people? Do I want people to have that kind of control over my reactions and emotions? Do I want to be someone who shares happiness with others all the time?

People often say to me, "Aviva, you know, I've had a lot of negative experiences happen to me and I'm going through some tough times. Now you're just asking me to let all of that go and just 'be happy'?"

I know it sounds like an impossible order, but I can tell you, I've lived most of my life answering this question and getting my hands dirty in the muck of the world in the process.

I was born in Latvia, a country in Eastern Europe, in what was then the Soviet Union. My parents separated when I was six years old, with my father moving to Israel, and so I spent most of my early childhood with my mom and my grandparents. I didn't have a lot of friends growing up, so I didn't really get a chance to experience, early on, what it was like to have really close friends. Our family was very tight-knit, and they kept me sheltered from too much contact with others, for good reason. We were a Jewish family, and under Communist rule, you couldn't practice your religion openly, and always had to be careful about what you talked about in public, staying under the radar of the authorities. Eventually, our family wanted freedom. Freedom of choice and freedom of speech, and we decided that we should emigrate to Canada.

Our Limiting Beliefs

All right, so why am I sharing all of this with you? Simply, I want you to see how my own limiting beliefs came about, and what impact they had on my later life and on my relationships.

First, I was born into and raised in an environment where we could not express our deepest, fondest beliefs, and that repression creates a corresponding urge to act out. I learned to hold back parts of myself or risk getting hurt.

I then moved to a new country that was very different from my first home and had to deal with the rejection that nearly every immigrant faces when they first start out in their new lands. In this case, from those first few kids at school who made fun of me. It made me feel isolated, bullied, and it reinforced my low self worth from when I didn't get the affection and positive praise from my parents. I spent a lot of time trying to win the affection of my Mom, who was way too busy working to support us, and very rarely getting that acknowledgement. I "learned" that I didn't deserve love, affection, or attention.

Next, I finally found freedom and belonging with a group of kids who accepted me for who I was, but who were into some pretty destructive habits that I ended up taking on for myself so that I could fit in. I learned improper boundaries and unhealthy patterns.

Your limiting beliefs determine, in large part, how your romantic relationships go later in life. You may not always notice the connection between the past and the future, but they are interrelated when you really take the time to reflect on them. In my case, the limiting beliefs would, later on, cause me to do the following:

- Fall in love with a man who would leave me feeling alone in the relationship.
- Become involved with someone who cheated on me.
- Stay in a relationship without recognizing red flags.
- Allow people to take advantage of me or manipulate me to their advantage.
- Allow people to use me for their own needs, without considering my needs.

I share this because I do want you to understand that I have walked where you have walked, and where you may still be walking. I know what it feels like to have love go horribly wrong…and I know how to get out of that negative, dark hole that your spirit is trapped inside. Keep these experiences in mind as we delve further into this book. On top of that, I also suggest that you reflect on your own life and times, especially those early years, because that is where many of our profoundly limiting beliefs are born.

So, how do limiting beliefs work to sabotage your relationships, and how do you deal with them?

Let's quickly review our earlier conversation on control. If two people love each other and they want to stay together, they're going to stay together because they respect each other, love each other, accept each other, understand each other's needs, and value commitment. But if somebody has issues or has not done the work on themselves, they can walk any time or push you to walk out because of the unhealthy patterns. Let me make something very clear to you. The reality is that no matter what relationship you're in, romantic or not, anybody married or not, can walk away at any time. You have no control over what anyone else does, but you have control over yourself, how you treat others, how you allow others to treat you, and your commitments. People want to be together because they love each other and they make that choice. When we say that someone has issues, it's really another, less-fancy way of saying that they have limiting beliefs. They had painful experiences in their lives early on that taught them certain things about themselves and the world, whether true or false, and they make their decisions in their own lives (and love lives) based on them.

Indeed, most limiting beliefs are rooted in painful past experiences. Pain is always going to be around in life. It's how you choose to deal with that pain that really matters. If we did not experience pain, how would we appreciate the beautiful things that come into our lives? Dealing with pain involves becoming conscious of how life really works, as we discussed earlier, and putting your experiences into context. If you don't do that, your limiting beliefs will determine your behavior by default. Things will fall apart, and you'll have no idea why it keeps happening. It's all rooted in a desire to protect yourself from pain, even if that initial painful experience happened decades ago. And it effects how you view yourself, which can also sabotage your own health and happiness.

Let's say I want to find love, and that I haven't been able to find it, or at least, find a love that lasts. I may not be able to see that, as the late Dr. Wayne Dyer put it, that the "common factor in all of my past failed relationships is me." Because I don't recognize that, I think it's always someone else's problem. He was a jerk, or she was a cheater, or they had commitment issues, etc. The most common mistake we run into is that it's always the other person.

In reality, outside of cases of abuse and assault where the perpetrator is responsible for causing you harm, you end up in dysfunctional relationships because part of you is allowing yourself to put up with them in the first place. Instead of wondering what is wrong with the person because of their actions, try a different perspective. What is wrong with you that you're allowing this to happen over and over again? Have you ever thought about that?

Nobody can do anything to you unless you allow them to. The question, then, to ask yourself is, "what is it that I'm doing that's allowing you to treat me like that and why am I making this kind of behavior okay?" When you find your answer, when you uncover the limiting belief that has you making that experience possible and put a stop to it, you'll never tolerate that kind of disrespect ever again.

Or, say, if you're single, and you're just having rotten luck finding someone who'll go out with you. Everybody gets rejected daily (and not just in dating, but at work, at school, in business, and so on), but have you ever stopped and wondered, 'why am I taking it personally?' First of all, no one likes rejection, but there's something about romantic rejection that hurts more than not being able to close a sale or getting a bad mark on a paper. With just a little bit of reflection, you may realize that romantic rejection just hits something deep down that affects your confidence level. If you think about it even more, you'll see that the rejection touches on something that happened when you were a kid that caused you to feel less than whole. So now, years later, as an adult, when you ask someone out on a date and they turn you down, all of a sudden, you go back to feeling like that hurt school-kid.

Often, the limiting beliefs come from our parents, but not in the way that you might think.

Back in my rebel teenage years, my Mom was very much an old-school parent. In many Soviet countries, and even in Russia and Latvia today, many parents instill in their kids the same fears that their parents had instilled in them. It can go back generations. One day, I rolled into the house late at night after an outing with my crew, and my Mom and my aunt were upset with me. "You keep this up," said Mom, "you're gonna end up a nobody!" Keep in mind, if you were a fly on the wall in that room during that conversation, you might have thought that they were screaming at me, but in fact, this is simply the average voice level for Latvian elders. They weren't trying to abuse me, though, they were simply trying to warn me of the consequences of my actions. What they were trying to say, of course, was that they wanted me to be happy, or wanted me to be successful, but that's not how they were taught to speak by their parents.

And how do you think that made me, the little rebel, react? From this moment I became ambitious, always striving to prove them wrong. I simply kept doing what I was doing. No one else was going to tell me what to do! This was Canada, a free country, and there were my friends who understood me! An ambitious and tenacious spirit was born and I no longer wanted to fail because if I did, they would be right. I ended up creating my own destructive habit, just to say "ha! You can't tell me what to do and I will prove you wrong!"

Reconditioning Limiting Beliefs

Why are people workaholics? Why are people always going after more when they're already so powerful and successful? What makes them drive and drive and drive, and no matter what you give them, they want to drive and drive for more? Simple, they're still proving a point from when they were a little kid.

Because somebody told them they weren't good enough. Because somebody told them they couldn't.

From that moment, you become somebody that is going to do everything in their power to show their critics otherwise. That's how that person becomes ambitious. That notion is a seed that gets planted way back then that turns into ambition later in life. Of course, there are parents who support and build their kids' confidence for them to become successful as well, and that's wonderful. But all too often, parents will cause their children to develop limiting beliefs without even meaning to, sometimes with dramatic results later in life.

While this seems like a great way to be successful – it definitely explains the motivation of many successful people - there is a price. When those people fail at something, or something doesn't go their way, the initial lack of self-worth that was around when that seed was planted kicks right back in. Then the self-sabotage begins. In relationships, it looks like getting involved with the wrong partners, getting into fights over trivial matters, lying, cheating, in some extreme cases, mental and physical abuse. All stemming from the original limiting beliefs and unhealthy experiences that our parents had to endure during their lives.

What do we do, then?

You have to reprogram yourself and recondition those imprinted beliefs, and do it in a way that keeps you ambitious, but also reminds you to be a human being from time to time. That's where the work is: exposing the negative old beliefs and experiences and the habits that come from them, and creating new beliefs and patterns that will give you what you want (and help you raise your children in a healthy way).

It's like saying a prayer. When your prayer gets answered, you start to believe more. You begin to believe more, and before you know it, your whole belief system changes. Better yet, you start having experiences in your life – whirlwind romances that are healthy and delightful, better conversations, fun times – and the results then reinforce the belief. The downward spiral becomes an upward spiral, and though that's not to say that there isn't always some work to be done here and there, it does mean that you can transform yourself and thereby your hopes for love and fulfillment.

The Conversation You Need to Have with Yourself

Now that you have an understanding or awareness of what kind of world we live in and how to interpret it, what kind of life do you want to create for yourself within that world without having it negatively affecting you? If you've been praying for a better life, in the next chapter, we're going to start distinguishing those limiting beliefs and replacing them with beliefs and practices that will start you on the way to that brilliant future.

The conversation that you need to have with yourself is, "how badly do you want this happiness?" Are you ready for commitment? Are you prepared to build integrity? Are you willing to receive the love for yourself to take the necessary steps to get that happiness?

Let's create the vision, establish our word and commitment, and let's start getting to the work.

Chapter 2

IT'S NEVER
TOO LATE

*"If you change nothing …
nothing will change"*

N ow that you have a little more insight about how the world is around us, the question is now: knowing that we only have one shot at this thing called "life," how would you like to exist within this world? What kind of life do you choose for yourself?

If you had your own personal genie, what would your wish list be? Would you wish for more money? Would you want to be with the woman or the man of your dreams? Would you want to be somebody who lived a particular lifestyle or looked a certain way?

It's essential to make this clear, this isn't about perfection. This is about finding fulfillment, confidence, and happiness from here on out.

If you're reading this, realistically, you might not be exactly where you envisioned yourself or your life to be. No one is exactly how they conceive themselves to be. You may think it's too late for you, and you may have been operating in that mindset for a long time. The limiting belief that it's too late to change or improve things can end with you indulging in any number of unhealthy choices and behaviors. You might just stop exercising one day, for example, or give up on a proper diet. You might only decide that you're unlucky in love and that no one will find you attractive, so you stop looking. Maybe you're tired of the dating scene and all the issues that exist in people who don't know what they want. Maybe you're heartbroken, in a funk, or dealing with some depression or mental health issues. All of these factors and more could have you thinking to yourself, "You know what? This is just as good as it gets and I should be grateful for the little bit that I do have, even though I know that there's more." Over time, all of those thoughts in your mind pile up.

Adults always ask kids, "who do you want to be when you grow up?" You might have said "I want to be a race car driver," or "musician," "fireman," "police officer," "lawyer," "teacher,"

"doctor," or what have you. If someone were to ask you that question now, you'd probably laugh. You might be everything that you said you wanted to be, or you might be the complete opposite, wondering how you ever thought you could be those other things in the first place.

One question you were probably never asked as a kid or as a grownup, however, is who do you want to be right now, and in the years to come?

I'm assuming that if you're reading this, you've lived a few decades on this planet. That's plenty of time to have developed many limiting beliefs, but also to have dreamed about what is possible for you. As I noted earlier, whether you're twenty or eighty years old, you might have decided at some point that it's too late for change or improvement. Your plans went one way and your life the other, and with them, your dreams. Or maybe you had it all, and you lost it all, and now you feel defeated, so why bother?

I'm here to tell you that you can change your mind and your life right now. This is your moment of truth, the time for the conversation with yourself, no matter how hard things may feel, or how confused or discouraged you may feel. It's an opportunity for you to make your very first right decision! The decision to want more, go after more, and to understand all the whys because you deserve it!

"You don't always have to be great to start...but you have to start to be great!"

Before we get into our first steps toward the beginning of your life's new chapter, you will need a journal to stay organized with the lists and commitments. We will stay on track together, and if you allow me, I will guide you.

This is your first exercise: Take a day, a week, a month, or any amount of time necessary to really think about the kind of life you wish to lead. How do you want to be treated by others? What kind of self-respect are you willing to live by? Do you know what your boundaries should be when it comes to people and relationships (you need to remember, they will have their limitations as well, as we all live in our own worlds)? What are your deal breakers when it comes to romantic relationships?

In the next few pages, this is also where we start creating our lists to stay organized with our thoughts and commitments.

When you're ready, I want you to make the following commitment to yourself. Say it out loud – no one else needs to be around – but say the following:

I [your name], hereby declare that, in spite of any disappointments which I may have endured or experienced in this unpredictable world, I deserve and choose a life of happiness and substance. I commit to the process of becoming the best version of myself and loving myself first. I choose to create my own beautiful world of happiness and fulfillment on my own time and terms with integrity, so that I may live the life I deserve and always wanted to live.

This is your commitment. Throughout the rest of this book, I'll be guiding you, but it begins with a promise. Following that, it's a matter of integrity.

What is Integrity, Anyway?

By now, if you've read any other self-help books, you've probably got a couple of ideas about what integrity is. In the world of personal growth, as reflected by such teachers as Anthony Robbins, T. Harv Ecker, or Werner Erhardt, integrity isn't defined as "ethics" or "morality ." You need those too, but often, we tend to put those two concepts together to mean the same thing.

Now, when I say "integrity," I mean, "wholeness and completeness ." The same way that a building needs integrity in all its bricks and foundations to stay standing so does a person when they make a commitment. They need to have integrity in their thoughts, words, and actions.

That's all very fancy and esoteric, but what does that look like in practice? Well, let me give you an example.

Suppose you make a commitment that you want to be in the best possible shape you can. And, knowing that you've set this as your goal, you come home one day. You're tired, you went to the gym this morning, you've been good all week long . But, oops, you forgot to take the chicken out to thaw! Now you have to wait a while before you can have dinner. You check the fridge, there are no leftovers. What do you decide to do? You open up Skip the Dishes on your phone, and an hour later, you're eating greasy Chinese food which basically undoes the caloric deficit for the day.

Now, that's not an awful thing. You can probably recover from that the next day. But in that moment, you stepped out of your commitment to do what it takes to be in the best possible shape you can be. And in so doing, you put yourself out of integrity. You've chosen one of the foundations of the building that you're creating called "physical vitality" and knocked it down. Putting it back up is as simple as making sure that you have a healthy meal, or at least a healthy ingredient prepared for you so that when you come home, you can cook right away.

That's just one small example. Another slightly more serious example could be giving someone your word or promise and not following through without any kind of communication or explanation. We understand that things can get in the way; however, this will break down the trust and respect people have for you.

So, what does this have to do with re-creating yourself? Actually, it has everything to do with it. It's these small steps that add up over time.

As actor Will Smith recounted when his father had asked him and his brother as children to help build a wall for his business. Will's father had taught him that it wasn't about making the biggest wall, but about "laying each brick as perfectly as a brick can be laid, and you keep doing that, and eventually you have a wall ."

If you want to live a fulfilling life, you need commitment and integrity. Your integrity is built on hundreds of little bricks in the form of the decisions and actions that you take, every day, for however long it takes, to transform your life. Physical health, of course, is just one area. Your commitment to your word can also transform your relationships, your job and money, all these other aspects of what makes your optimal life. Integrity is a decision based in aligned thoughts, words, and actions, and as we all know, actions speak louder than just words.

If It's That Simple, Why Doesn't Everyone Do It?

This is as simple as you can imagine, but it's not easy. If you've ever tested out a diet for a week or started a new workout regimen, you know it's tough to resist the temptation to stray. Your commitment will be tested almost as soon as you make it. It's up to you to build your muscle for "follow through ." The way that you follow through is to keep your commitments. Of course, we are not perfect, and things happen along the way that is out of our control. It takes practice, and over time, you'll get it right.

The things that knock most people out of integrity, though – that cause them to skip that workout, go back to that awful ex-lover, or tolerate being treated like garbage at their job – are one or more limiting beliefs, as we've discussed. The limiting beliefs will act up when you least suspect. They can look like all the things that we mentioned – breaking a diet, going back to an ex, etc.

Here's the interesting part about limiting beliefs. Because they are subconscious (that is, you're not consciously aware of them), as soon as you become aware of them through the exercises we're about to do, they will cease to function. That doesn't mean that they go away, but for the time that you're consciously-aware of them, you know you are empowered to make different choices in your actions. Your awareness of your limiting beliefs takes them out of operation and gives you the opportunity to make a new choice that's in alignment with the commitment that you just made.

Decluttering Your Emotional Mind

Limiting beliefs are like junk. They accumulate in your unconscious over time. Unlike boxes and furniture that collect dust in your basement, this kind of junk actively gets in your way, sabotaging your decisions and tripping you up. Ever wander into a living room at night and find yourself tripping over toys or other objects in the dark? That's what your limiting beliefs do in your relationships. How are you supposed to identify them and clean them up if you are not even aware of them? That's why it's essential to understand where we come from (how the world works and how it has affected us) before we can recognize and make decisions towards where we are going.

Decluttering the subconscious of your limiting beliefs is the first step in transforming your relationships. But after decades of just being alive, you've probably got hundreds of them. How can you clean it all up?

Well, for starters, you can't clean up all of them. This isn't about obtaining a state of purity. You'll always have something happening in your subconscious that you can't identify or control. If you tried to do that, you would be overwhelmed right from the get-go! First, we need to slowly become conscious of them and recognize them when they pop up. Once you start identifying your patterns, it becomes easier to deal with on the spot.

Also, if you've experienced significant traumas - especially those involving violence and sexual trauma of any kind - you would do well to see a professional therapist or counselor. They can help you heal some of the deepest wounds that self-directed work such as what we're doing here may not be able to reach. At times, one might not be able to identify the clues of the subconscious mind, and you are not able to clearly grasp the level of the negative impact that you may have endured during your childhood. You might not even be aware of it. But if you sense that there could be something substantial there, I would suggest seeing a professional to ensure that you have overturned every rock and understand the level of therapy that you need. What we are doing in this book is a self-help process and not clinical therapy.

What you can do, however, is keep a list. In fact, the list is all you need to start to declutter. I'm going to show you how you can take action in just a moment.

Why are lists so important? Daily, we have so many things that we have to get done. We have to get groceries, we have to pick up dry cleaning, we have to send a proposal to somebody, we have to answer calls, and although they might be these tiny little things and you might be this brilliant person who thinks you got it all under control, you'll likely forget something, right? Then you have all the other areas of your life to organize, figure out, fix, or control such as projects, work, kids, relationships, and so on. And now we need to go back to our past and try to figure out our shit ourselves.

I mean, where's the escape hatch, right?

So, to make sure that you are efficient, and not stressed or anxious or overwhelmed carrying that load, it's better to put it somewhere else for safe-keeping that you can refer to. You're reassured that it's somewhere safe and you know all those things are covered for you to prioritize and tackle when ready. You don't have to worry about remembering them. Right?

List-making is actually a mild form of therapy as well as a great tool to stay organized and on top of things. Lists clear and declutter your mind so you can feel lighter, be productive, and stay on top of your responsibilities and commitments. This is also how you declutter your limiting beliefs. If you've ever decluttered your house, then you know just how good it feels when it's all over. It's like you have a new home! (In fact, decluttering your physical living space is one crucial step to creating that beautiful future, which we'll discuss in a later chapter).

List-making allows you to practice letting go of things. And, as part of decluttering involves donating simple and sometimes valuable items which you no longer need, it also allows you to give to others who are less fortunate. Which automatically reinforces your compassion, kindness, and efficiency in the work that you're doing (we will be talking about this in detail in the chapters ahead).

The Wish List: Who Do You Choose to Be?

Now that we have a clear understanding of what lists are for, actually putting it on paper is the first manifestation of the life you want to have in reality. That piece of paper you're holding in your hand? That's a part of the new life that you're creating for yourself!

So, we come back to it: who do you choose to be? Take a few minutes right now and think about it. Don't worry, you don't have to be absolutely perfectly clear about your vision right at this second. Wherever you're starting from works.

One great way to go about doing this is journaling. It doesn't have to be a fancy, leather backed diary. A simple coil notebook that you can pick up from Wal-Mart and a ballpoint pen will do the trick. This is where you'll put your lists, and this one, the Wish List, will be your first.

Take some time and answer the following questions. Create your wish list specifically around your dreams and answers around the example questions below.

- If I could have anything in the world, what would that be? (Would it be a sexy, fit body? Would it be better health? More confidence? Better friends?)
- What kind of person do I want to be?
- Do I want to be a positive person? Do I want to laugh a lot? Do I want to be kind? Do I want to be judgmental? Stubborn, or open-minded? Boring, or fun? Cheap, or generous? Do I want people to respect me and look up to me?

- What kind of life do I wish to lead? Do I want a simple life, or extravagance? Do I want healthy balance in my life? Do I want to travel? Do I want a relationship, or do I just want to have fun?

These questions may seem simple, but it is powerful. A colleague of mine who did this exercise after speaking with me answered that he'd love to travel every year or twice a year, not at all for business, but just for pleasure. "Just to go and explore," he said to me. As he reflected further, he also discovered that he wanted to live on a farm that he would use as a venue for weddings and special events, something that he'd envisioned years before, but never took it seriously. It turns out this was something that he had deeply wanted more than he'd considered, even to himself! He also realized a deep desire to rescue unwanted dogs and help them find homes. Again, something else he'd toyed with, but never tried to make happen.

Take some time to really drill down into your fondest desires and see what comes up. Write them down.

Using my colleague as an example, he came up with wanting to be "100% comfortable in his own skin, to look young and confident. Healthy, happy, and energized." He wanted to live close to his friends in a community where everyone knew each other and looked out for one another. As well, he desired a relationship with a wonderful woman with whom he had common long-term goals and unique chemistry.

What I believe to be most important about my colleague's answers, though, is his last one. In terms of how he wanted to feel in general, he said simply, "confident ." This is the key!

Confidence is the piece of the puzzle that a lot of us are missing. The confidence that comes from feeling good in your skin and having a remarkable life.

Even if you don't want the exact same things, what most people have in common is that desire for confidence.

Distinguishing the Limiting Beliefs

As you go about this exercise, if you're not sure or you have trouble with this, start paying attention to your feelings. As you visualize the qualities that this person would have – say, confidence in the dating world, a leader in their workplace, a beautiful home that energizes and empowers them to feel good – notice when you start feeling inexplicably sad or downhearted. This is a good indicator of heartbreak or attachment to negative influence, which may have happened in the past. Maybe it was someone you have given up on becoming, but who you still wish to be. Go ahead and think of one of your wildest, fondest aspirations that you've since given up on. That feeling right there, in your chest? That's what we call "heartbreak" or "pain."

Heartbreak can feel like an emotional scab or a scar, tender to the touch, and in our day to day life, we may have developed a habit of trying our best not to think about it. As performance coach Mel Robbins notes in her TED Talk, it's probably a dream or a wish that "you've convinced yourself that you're fine not having." And it makes sense. When we feel something painful, the natural tendency is to try to distract our attention away from it so the feeling will go away. Most people who are not aware of those limiting beliefs will run from pain or fear. We'll go do the dishes or throw ourselves back into work, become depressed or isolated, basically turn our attention away from what still lives inside of us as a future waiting to be born.

Let yourself, just for this moment, believe that it is still possible. (Remember, giving up on possibility is a limiting belief.) Just allow yourself to enjoy the idea of being that person.

Almost immediately, you'll feel resistance. As you journal, take note of the words and feelings that come up. These are what your limiting beliefs sound like. They could be something like

"Oh, it's not possible!" or "you're too old/too fat/too stupid to try it now" or "you don't deserve to be that happy because of [insert past mistake or incident here] ." Write all of those down, too.

When you're finished, take a look. Go through and circle all of those limiting beliefs. In the next chapter, we're going to sort them into their own lists and then begin to take the actions necessary to renovate your life.

Chapter 3

DECLUTTERING YOUR CLOSET AND YOUR HOME

"Change your thoughts and you change your world."

NORMAN VINCENT PEALE

N ow that you have had the conversation with yourself about what kind of person you truly are and wish to be, and what kind of life you want, we can start putting things in motion.

Remember what I said earlier, that we don't truly understand how the world and the Universe operate? When you make a commitment to transform an aspect of your life, the Universe immediately starts working in your favor. As you go through these lists, every so often, take a look at your life. To declutter, we need to acknowledge what is not working in your life, or not working as well as you would like. For that to happen, you need to write them down in great detail.

The decluttering of your life begins here!

The first thing we'll tackle is creating our lists so we can stay organized. After we create our lists, we start executing the declutter of one category of life at a time.

Here are the lists that you'll need to create (templates for these lists are available at the end of this chapter):

- Your Vision/Wish List
- Declutter and Unfinished Projects List for Your Home
- Friends Lists
- Health and Wellness List

In addition to these, be sure to add any other list that you feel is important to you, such as "find a life partner" or "meet someone special" or "learn great dating techniques ." Just write them down in your wish list. Just wait until you start checking off your boxes! It is so much fun and feels so good to know you are growing and moving forward. As I always say, upward and onward!

Though it may not seem like it at this very moment, this is a magic formula, so it's absolutely essential that you complete the lists in this order. As you go about your decluttering, you'll start to notice the transformations already beginning to happen.

Decluttering Your Home

We're going to begin with your home space.

The reason we declutter our home first is because this is our personal space where we spend most of our time. Before we declutter anything else internally, this has to be the first place we tackle in order for us to consistently reinforce the positive work we will be doing on our mind and body. We need good energy, happy and bright surroundings in our immediate environment where we feel safe and happy before we start to work on ourselves. Every time you open your door, you will feel the brightness you created no matter what happened that day, good or bad.

Obviously, whether you live in a bachelor studio apartment or a mansion with many rooms, your home space is the most prominent physical transformation you can make right now to increase your power and your sense of solitude and positive reinforcement. As anyone who's ever moved houses numerous times knows, we accumulate a lot of clutter as we go through the years. Some of it we keep and we don't even know why!

This isn't to say that you shouldn't keep all those childhood pictures or those keepsakes, trophies, those gifts from your grandparents long since passed. We're not talking about those: they're the things that make up an essential component of who you are as a person. No, I'm not talking about the extra set of steak knives that you bought on sale, thinking you'd use them, but never opened. I'm talking about that corner of your basement den that just seems to attract things to it like a magnet. I'm talking about the coffee table gathering dust in the attic that you only kept because you thought it would be useful.

Material things accumulate over time, and that creates congestion in your sense of space. One of the things you need to understand about how the Universe works is the degree to which everything is a form of energy. When you keep stuff, that is mostly you keeping old energy, and that old energy may be attached to some periods of your life or experiences that you've had where you learned limitations. By keeping that energy around in your physical space, you're giving energy to your limiting beliefs, continuing to provide them with power. There's an intuitive understanding of this even in the pop culture that doesn't talk about spiritual things. Whenever somebody burns their wedding dress after they've gotten divorced, for example, what they're doing is getting rid of energy from the failed marriage that could legitimately cripple their future relationships.

It's not just about the stuff that you keep, either: it's the stuff that needs fixing. That shaky doorknob that you've just sort of been putting up with the past few years? That's one. That microwave that you haven't cleaned since two girlfriends ago?

That's another. And when was the last time you changed your furnace filter?

All of those things add up, becoming sources of irritation that cause you to leak some of your manifesting power. Irritation doesn't seem like much, but it's still restrictive negative energy.

It's a small problem that just causes a lot of resentment and overall grouchiness that diminishes your positivity. Worse yet, these little irritations drain you, leaving you feeling disconnected from the Universe and disempowered.

I'm a firm believer in proceeding in a logical, systematic way when it comes to decluttering. If you don't take a sensible approach, you'll overwhelm yourself and then get nothing done.

With that in mind, within your Home List, I want you to make the following sub-lists (where applicable):

- *Garbage*: This for everything you would get rid of without any hesitation that has no value for yourself or anyone else.
- *Donate*: This is for all of the clothes you've not worn for between 6 months to a year, that no longer fit, or are out of style. This also applies to other items as well (such as trinkets, pieces of furniture, books, old appliances, and so on).
- *Garage Sale*: : This list is for clothing and other items that you know have a higher value, or are in excellent condition, such that you can sell them and make a small amount of money. Whether you want to sell or donate them is up to you, but if you feel that they could be worth some money, add them to this list.
- *Storage*: This is for everything that you want to keep, but would rather not re-clutter your home space with, that you would like to utilize in the future (say, when you get a larger home), or that you would like to keep in the family (say, by giving to your children).

Depending on where you live, there are many services such as 1-800-GOT-JUNK, or other private organizations who will come to your house and take everything away for you. They will drop your items off to the appropriate locations.

You don't need to get too crazy with the details. There's no need to keep a detailed itemized list of every object you come across. Instead, allocate them into piles within each category. For your garage sale and donation piles, put those objects into plastic bins, which you can purchase at most retailers and are easy to store until you drop them off or sell them at your garage sale.

For your storage items, such as old pictures and other sentimental objects that don't necessarily fit with the decor you are trying to create, you can also keep these in bins wherever you see fit. You can reorganize your basements and attics, for example, to accommodate these items in a way that doesn't lead to more clutter like you had before. This way, your space will maintain a sense of order and openness.

Create a checklist of the areas in your house that you're going to tackle in order, and do each of them one at a time. Once you've decluttered your room and put your items in a bin, designate them according to the proper sublist, and set them aside in your basement or garage.

Finally, set a deadline for when you will have it all taken away by a service or when you will drop them off, and start designating your rooms according to an order that works for you.

You're probably looking at this right now and thinking "Ugh! That's so much work! Why do we have to do it like this?"

As I said before, I work logically and with good reason. There is a method to my madness. Once we take care of all the little things, we can then move on to bigger things, the grand things, of our lives. This will create an order. If we've done all the little things, we've now optimized ourselves to really focus on what matters.

The Decluttering Process

If you can, clear one day in your schedule to focus on decluttering without having to leave your house; otherwise, just do what you can when you can. Make sure you have enough garbage and recycling bags on hand and a dust mask. You can choose to declutter one room a day or one a week, depending on what suits you best.

Re-create your home based on how you want to feel in that space. For example, if you're somebody who entertains a lot, then your kitchen, dining, and family rooms can be turned into a fun space suited to entertaining dinner guests and small parties, as well as a cozy environment.

You can go from simple changes - such as rearranging your furniture - to a full renovation. It depends on how far you want to take it, which may be different for you than others. But if you're going to keep it simple and just make your home a cozier, more comfortable place suited to your personality, all it would take is a simple rearrangement of furniture or a splash of modern colors on a wall. You can add a few extra pillows on your bed, maybe a funky window treatment, some candles, flowers, and greenery, and voila!

While this is a very general guideline, here are a few specific areas where you might give some extra thought:

Closet - This is the first place you should start because it's the most intimate part of your living space and a source of a lot of leftover negative energy that holds you back.

Take a look at your wardrobe. If you're at home right now, whether you have ten outfits or a thousand, how much of what you wear is older than one year? Think about this: most of us buy our clothes to look good. Not just that, but the clothes that we have need to feel good as well. As they say, before you can get your head right, you need to get your threads right. So, go through what you have in your closets and drawers right now. Look for what's older than one year. When you've sorted them, I want you to take them and put them in a donation bag. You're getting rid of them.

When you're decluttering the things that surround you, because we have such a hard time letting go of things, it's much easier to do so knowing that you're helping somebody else by donating to someone less fortunate. Those clothes, furniture pieces, and other items that you've been keeping around because you remember how much you spent on them won't go to waste. Better yet, by helping to create abundance for others, you'll cultivate a feeling of generosity, kindness, compassion in your own heart, which feels wonderful and adds to your own positive energy. It will bring even more positive energy back to you, because, as we say, what goes around comes around!

You're not throwing them out unless you have to. What you're doing is taking what's old - representing your past self and that previous energy - and you're going to turn it into something new for somebody else, someone who doesn't necessarily have the same means as you do. That's why we're donating it to a thrift shop or to a charity that can give these clothes to people less fortunate. What you're then doing is adding energy to somebody else while also creating a vacuum of energy that will allow new clothes, new outfits, new looks to come in. With the ever-changing fashion trends, we always need to go shopping, which we will also talk about when we talk about Self Image later in this book.

Why does this matter? Because how you present your new self to the world matters. It'll determine first impressions, but most importantly, it'll show to the world that you've transformed. You're going to feel transformed by the end of this process.

Why do we hold onto old clothes? Well, some of us who want to lose weight hope that we'll someday fit into favorite clothing items again. What tends to happen, though, for those people, is that when they do finally fit back into that dress, or can eventually buckle that old pair of pants, they feel that they want something new. There's always that little feeling of "well, I went through all this just to put on these old pants?" As a friend of mine once said, it's like putting old plates on a new car. It doesn't feel that great. Sometimes, you just want something brand, spanking new.

What do you keep? Obviously, keep the essentials that you're still using every day for work, school, or what have you. If you have a favorite suit jacket, little black dress, or any other item that makes you feel empowered and attractive when you wear it, keep it.

Apply the law of "hell, yeah!" to decluttering your closet. If you see an item that you already know that you love, hold onto it. Everything else that isn't an immediate "hell, yeah!" in your mind let it go! If you have to think about it for a really long time and you can't decide, then it should probably go to somebody who would really love it. There are no "maybes" in this process, treat every "maybe" as a "no."

Be brave! Anything that you haven't touched in a year that isn't an absolute favorite get it gone! Anything that you're only keeping around because you paid a lot of money when you first got it, donate it.

In fact, donate your high-value clothes to charity or a second-hand shop. You'll help someone else who's less fortunate feel as though they've hit the jackpot when they find the comfortable dress that you don't need anymore! And don't worry, as you go through this process, you may find that you'll suddenly have some more money coming into your life to replace your old high-cost items with something new!

Bedroom - Once you've sorted your closet, let's take a look at the rest of your bedroom. First, look at the general layout: how does everything make you feel? Your bedroom should be a place of solace, safety, and rest. If you're not getting those vibes from your room as it is now, try to find out just what about your current setup could be causing that sense of unease.

Like the rest of your home, rearrange your room with the personality that best represents you. Men are different than women. Men tend to like a more masculine feel (cooler colors, deeper tones, modern, futuristic furniture, etc .), but of course, everyone has their own tastes. In my opinion, there should always be a touch of something that would make a woman feel comfortable if you're in a relationship or looking to meet someone.

Make sure to include some extra pillows on the bed, maybe a few plants, and some candles for those romantic moments.

The sky's the limit. Hire a designer or simply look at some pictures (a beautiful interior design website called Houzz .com can provide you with some inspiring ideas). See what appeals to you, and maybe replicate it. Figure out what your level of affordability is and make the best of it.

Kitchen - The kitchen is one of those places where we're most prone to having junk pile up because kitchen utensils are cheap and readily available (think back to the steak-knives I mentioned before). Often, we buy new items to replace older items that we never end up throwing out. For many people, there's a strange sentimental attachment to old knives and spoons that just means they clutter up our drawers and cupboards. Look around. How often do you cook? What do you tend to make? Do you really need three different kinds of wooden spoons? Go through each drawer and cupboard and be relentless. If you see, say, an old, rusty knife that you keep telling yourself you're going to have sharpened, but haven't done it in three years, just get rid of the damn thing already!

And don't forget to clean out your fridge, freezer, and pantry. You'd be surprised how quickly canned goods expire. Plus, when we start talking about self-image, you might find that you'll be changing your diet anyway.

Garage and Basement - As we go about this process, we'll need to create some space for the items we intend to keep (or at least for the time being until we take it away). Designate an area in your house where you feel comfortable to hold your items temporarily. For myself, I would most likely choose to keep them in my garage or basement.

The garage is another place where we tend to put things we don't want to deal with and then forget about them. Unless you're a car enthusiast and spend a lot of time fixing up your ride (in which case, your garage is probably already super-organized and neat), it's more likely you only go into your garage when you're going out or coming home, or when you have to put out garbage and recycling . Make sure to clear away as much clutter as you can to make room for what you want to store.

Unfinished Projects - All those little things that you've neglected to do, create some time to do them and get them done. Fix the leaks in the shower, weed your garden, patch up the cracks in the walls, and so on. If you're not terribly handy, call someone who can get it all done for you. And then, check it off your list!

Creating a New Space

Once you've finished your decluttering, take a look around. How do you feel now? If you've been thorough and followed the steps as I've presented them here, you should have a distinct feeling of "Whew! What a relief!" Now there's more room for you to re-shape your living environment in a way that empowers you and fuels that vision of a higher version of yourself. If you're feeling particularly adventurous, you can choose to renovate your home. This is a big undertaking, and it is fraught with risks, but with the right guidance and expert advice, you can have the home of your dreams without having to move!

First, of course, dust, sweep and mop all of those new empty places. You're not only cleaning but getting rid of the last bits of that old energy. Now that you've done that, your living space has become an empty canvas. You can paint anything you want!

Your life is now your fresh, new canvas, so go nuts and have fun creating something that suits your personality and how you wish to feel in your space.

THE WISH LIST

If I could have anything in the world, what would that be? (e.g. a sexy, fit body, better health, confidence, great friends, etc.)

- ....
- ....
- ....
- ....
- ....
- ....

What kind of person do I want to be (e.g. positive, a leader, happy)? How do you want people to know you? List the qualities you desire:

- ....
- ....
- ....
- ....

- ....
- ....
- ....
- ....
- ....
- ....
- ....
- ....
- ....
- ....

What do I want in my life? What kind of life do I wish to lead? (e.g. simple/extravagant, travel-filled, single, relationship, etc.)

- ....
- ....
- ....
- ....
- ....
- ....
- ....
- ....
- ....
- ....
- ....
- ....
- ....

LIST FOR DECLUTTERING YOUR HOME

Do one area at a time that fits your schedule until you are done:
- ☐ Bedroom and Bedroom Closet
- ☐ Other Bedrooms
- ☐ Basement
- ☐ Garage
- ☐ Attic
- ☐ Bathrooms
- ☐ Kitchen
- ☐ Living room/Dining room

For each area, include this sub list to sort and label your items:
- Garbage Removal - This goes into garbage bags.
- Donation - This goes in donation boxes or garbage bags for donation.
- Storage - This goes into boxes, bins, etc.
- (Optional): Garage Sale

LIST OF UNFINISHED PROJECTS

Home Care (e.g. Fixing things around the house, garage, yard, renovations, etc.)

- ☐ ....
- ☐ ....
- ☐ ....
- ☐ ....
- ☐ ....

☐ ....
☐ ....

Personal (e.g. journals, paintings, writing, crafting, gardening, etc.)

- ....
- ....
- ....
- ....
- ....
- ....
- ....

HEALTH AND WELLNESS LIST

Goals
- Desired weight: ....
- Desired pants/dress size: ....
- Desired shirt size: ....

Dietary Goals:
☐ Clean out fridge/cupboards of all sugary/unhealthy foods
☐ Purchase healthy snacks
☐ Create/purchase a meal plan from a certified nutritionist

Fitness Goals
- Number of cardio workouts per week: ......
- Number of resistance workouts per week: ....

- Do I want to hire a personal trainer? ☐Y ☐N
- Do I want to buy a gym membership? ☐Y ☐N

What Types of Physical Activities Do I Want to Do? (e.g. Zumba, cycling, hiking, jogging, krav maga, Tai Chi, yoga, etc.).

- ....
- ....
- ....
- ....
- ....
- ....
- ....
- ....

Self Image Items
  - ☐ Shopping for new wardrobe
  - ☐ Mani-Pedi
  - ☐ Hair stylist appointment
    Do I want to hire a style consultant? ☐Y ☐N

Chapter 4

DECLUTTERING YOUR FRIENDS

"No one can make you feel inferior without your consent."

ELEANOR ROOSEVELT

So now you've optimized your home. In the next chapter, we will look at decluttering your friends and family, and the negative energy that some people carry that affects us. Don't worry, we're not going to do anything crazy or drastic, but we're going to help you tweak your friendships and the people who surround you so that you will not be affected by any negative, limiting beliefs that they may impose on you.

When I talk about decluttering your friends, this is the process of transformation where I usually get the most resistance from my clients. On the surface, it sounds like I'm suggesting that you get rid of your friends, or that you turn away from your friends in their times of need and think only about yourself. That's not what this is at all.

By "decluttering your friends," I am proposing that you simply begin to manage your relationships in a way that empowers you, rather than disempowers you.

This is part of the process that I like to call "building up your armor," which I will go into more detail on shortly.

We are always surrounded by people who we call our friends, colleagues, or acquaintances, and we have relationships to a certain degree with all of them, some closer than others. These people all have an impact on our thought processes through our interactions with them. They can come to us for advice, suggestions, sharing their life experiences and beliefs systems with us, information that they think they know (and what they think they know but don't really know), and we absorb everything that we get from them. We then decide if we agree with it or not. Sometimes, we'll take their advice or follow their guidance. If there's something that we don't know, we tend to listen to others more, assuming that, at times and on specific subjects, they may know more than we do.

All these little things get into our heads, and we think we're doing the right thing by listening to them. Sometimes, the people closest to you will give you advice that's not good for you because they're associating their own experiences and projecting them onto you. When we are not aware of our limiting beliefs, it's almost inevitable for us to act and react in our relationships. We then run with that and create habits for ourselves, many of which are not necessarily good for us.

It's good to compartmentalize these people and decide for yourself what you're willing to take in and not take in because, in the end, it will affect you and the quality of your life. As a wise person once said, other people don't have to live with the consequences of the advice they give you. No matter what kind of relationships you have, they should be built on mutual respect and you should have the choice of how much of yourself you are willing to share with each one of them, depending on how they treat you.

Consider that the words of wisdom from teachers such as Napoleon Hill – namely, that we become like the people closest to us - have a basis in reality. Think about it: who do you see daily? It could be your relatives and family, friends, and acquaintances, or people from work. We have to compartmentalize these people and figure out who we should and shouldn't listen to.

We know how to keep the people who aren't close to us at bay. If you have a rival at work, for example, or a neighbor who you don't like and don't get along with, you know how to identify and avoid those individuals.

The human mind is very skilled in dealing with threats. In fact, according to many neuroscientists, there's a big part of the brain that's responsible for your limiting beliefs and is almost wholly devoted to protecting you. This is what some researchers call the "lizard brain" or the "animal brain." This is the brain that assesses a situation and decides whether or not you need to run and hide, or stay and fight (a.k.a. the "flight or fight response").

Managing that part of the brain and that part of your awareness is key to any kind of transformation that you're going to have. Because initially, the change will appear as a threat to your lizard brain, which will then put up all sorts of resistance in the form of disempowering stories, excuses, self-sabotage, and most of all, fear.

On the other hand, you also want to be able to protect your new beliefs, which requires some measure of diligence. To do that, you need to build up your armor.

Developing Your Armor by Managing Your Relationships

As Will Smith's character said in The Pursuit of Happiness, "if you've got a dream, you've got to protect it." Similarly, as you go about this process of decluttering and recreating your life in a way that is the most empowering version of you, you'll want to protect that dream while at the same time remaining open to transformation and positivity. You'll need to develop some armor. What that means is that as you manage your relationships, you may notice that some people trigger negative responses from you no matter what.

Have you ever had that one person - may be a relative - who, no matter what happens, has a way of getting under your skin when you least expect it? They just consistently find a way to undermine your confidence in yourself. Maybe they have a way of communicating and can't help but insult you by accident. No matter the reason, you know who these people are in your life. If you had them growing up, you probably had to deal with them in school under circumstances where you couldn't get away from them. When I was in school, I was bullied, and at the same time, I had to share the same classroom with them. As a functioning adult, however, you have more control over the people in your life than you might think. Even as adults, we might still sometimes insist on keeping people around who drain us for one reason or another ("but I've known him forever").

Who am I talking about here? They could be, but aren't limited to:

- People who find a way to make you feel less confident about yourself and your abilities.
- People who make you second-guess yourself and the decisions that you've made by always pointing out what's wrong with them. You'll recognize these people by their most common way of starting a sentence "The problem with that is...", or who tells you "don't do that!" when you share a new goal or dream. They may be your, friends, but have you noticed that there are people in your life who you can always count on to be negative?
- People who are terribly late or cancel last minute after you have made an effort or gone out of your way to

include them. If they don't respect your time, it means they don't respect you.

- People who continuously interfere with your relationships, such as over-bearing parents, in-laws, or jealous friends? Although we don't choose our families, we must learn how to deal or cope with what comes to us. You want to surround yourself with people that see the cup half full, not half empty.

- People who have a long history with you. For example, your parents, regardless of whether you're 5, 15, or 50 years old, will always see you as their child to some degree. This is just natural. What that means is that even though they may grow and adjust with you, and though they may see you become a fully-functioning adult with a career and place of your own, maybe a family, there's always going to be that part of them that never quite get used to the idea that you're all grown up .

Remember how we talked about people who lived in their own worlds? What happens with people who have known you for a long time is that, in their world, you are still that person you used to be, and there's very little you can do to change how they see you. As a character from the TV Show Arrested Development once remarked to his younger CEO sibling, "You're my brother, nothing you do will ever impress me."

Here's the tricky part: you know your enemies. It's your friends, the people closest to you, who can do the most damage. Your armor is always up against your known enemies and critics in your life. If you have a critic who you might encounter, you know what you're going to say to them. You'll defend your dream. You'll protect it because you rightly recognize the threat. That's your armor.

With your friends, however, the threat is less obvious. This is why, to build up your armor, we need to manage how much interaction you have with your friends. To do that, we're going to use our favorite tool, the List.

First, we create a list of the different types of people in our lives, then we create a list of the kind of relationship we want to have with them. (Again, I've enclosed a list template at the end of this chapter for your use).

Friend Categories

On your first list write down your **family members**, including in-laws if you have them.

Next, list your **closest friends** - your go-tos for advice, support, fun. These are the people who are always around in your life. They're the secret-keepers who you turn to when you're going through the worst times of your life, the ones who you would give your life for, and who would do the same for you. These could be people you might not always see every day, they could be separated by distance, maybe even thousands of miles away. Still, when you do reconnect it's like nothing ever happened, you pick up right where you left off no matter how long ago it was since you were face to face. These are definitely the people who would go in the close friends' category.

CHAPTER 4: DECLUTTERING YOUR FRIENDS

Then, write down your **acquaintances**. These can be people you like to spend time with once in a while who bring something to your relationships, but with whom you might not share intimate or sensitive details with of your life.

Finally, write down your **business and work colleagues** (if you associate with them outside of office hours). Who are the people who brighten your dreary days at the office?

On the second list, I want you to identify two types of people and sort the names from your first list into the category that suits them best.

- **People Who Lift Me Up (Family and Close Friends)**: These are people who, after you see them, you always leave feeling better for having seen them. They love you, they support you, tell you the truth, and even if you have disagreements on specific issues, they'll still be there for you. The best kind of friend you can have is someone who can break things down for you and help you see things that you potentially cannot see because of your own bias. The best thing they can say to you is, "I am always going to be honest with you, I'm always going to be here for you, and I'm always going to support you, no matter what you decide."

- **People Who Drag Me Down**: These are the people who only seem to find you when they need something. This is what some people call a "foul-weather friend." This is that person who, if they need to borrow $500, will seek you out. But if you ever need them for anything, your calls just go straight to voicemail. Sometimes its family or in-laws who make things difficult or challenging because there is less acceptance, or there is jealousy or favoritism. Or, maybe friends who call you for advice on a problem, and when you give them a solution, they make a commitment to take your advice but don't end up following it. A few months later, they're calling you again with the same problem. Often, they just want a shoulder to cry on, but the thing about a relationship is that there should be a give and take. These are the people who only take from you or forget to appreciate you, or take you for granted. You don't always want to spend your energy convincing somebody to be happy or coaching or giving therapy because it can be very draining. You cannot coach someone who is not coachable. What you want is somebody who's on the same playing field as you that's going to give you positive energy. You're going to provide them with positive energy in turn. Remember, it doesn't matter what kind of relationship you have - romantic or non-romantic - it's always a give and take.

- **Fun Acquaintances:** These are people who aren't as close as your close friendships and family, but who bring something positive to the table, something that fulfills a need that you have. These friends are a little bit more casual. Maybe they like to go out drinking, sleep around, party it up. You'd never bring them over to a classy cocktail party or have in-depth conversations with them, but when you're looking to head out on the town on Saturday night, you can call them up, and they'll say "yes."

- **Pain/Regret List:** Create a list of people or situations where you may have regret or pain. You cannot speak for anyone else, but when it comes to you and your life, it's vital to clear negative energy, forgive people and ask for forgiveness, and let go of past arguments no matter if you were right or wrong. If a relationship went sour and someone was hurt, say you're sorry for your part in it. Try to pay it forward with kindness to show integrity, class, and growth. Bring good energy back to yourself. This exercise is for you, not them. They don't need to like you, but they will respect you for this mature action. Respect goes much further in life than being liked.

Of course, real life is not always as simple where you can neatly slot the people you know into lists. Every now and then, your supportive friends will sometimes bring you down, and the friends who typically drag you down will surprise you by being there for you. Much of the time, different circumstances determine the dynamic of your friendships, which is why we're not just merely ending friendships (not yet, anyway).

With that in mind, take a look at your friend's lists and think, "when do I usually have the best times with these guys?"

You can have different friends in different categories, but you choose how to control your environment within those friendships. Maybe you have friends you feel are close, always supportive, and are always there for you. You have fun with them. You'd introduce them to your family, you'd bring them into your home.

You don't necessarily need to close any doors with people around you, but you do have control of how they affect you in your relationships with them. Who are your true supportive friends? Who are those who bring you down? And who are those in between?

Good Advice: A Guide to Sifting Through Your Friends

The best kind of advice that someone can give you is objective advice. This would come from someone supportive, but not overbearing, who knows how to guide you without prejudice. Here's an example: you're going through a tough breakup, and you go to your best friend. Let's say you tell them what happened, and they see how upset you are. They're probably going to give you advice that sounds like, "oh, you're so much better than them! Let that piece of shit go! You don't need them. Move on with your life!" Now, this friend is not in your situation, and they're not going through what you're going through, and most of all, they tend to forget that there are always two people in the relationship. The responsibility is on both of those people to take ownership of what they've created with each other and the situation they're in. Maybe in this particular situation, someone is not aware of their limiting beliefs.

Most of the time, people will give you advice based on the situations that they have been in. This is something that can be a good thing - they can relate to your pain and show compassion towards you - but at the same time, they're also projecting their experiences and limiting beliefs from their situation onto you.

Remember, they're living in their box-world with their own perspectives. Most of the time, those who give you advice don't really know the extent of your situation and how you got there, so how reliable can their advice be?

The best kind of advice is from someone neutral, who will give you advice but will think of both parties involved. These people would say, "I don't agree with what's happening, and I think there's another way to go about this. Still, I understand why you would be upset, it's not right, and I'm going to support you no matter what you do ." Those kinds of friends we keep closer to us as they add happiness to our lives. It's good to have a positive friendship and support system. Most of all, tell them about your transformation, they will be over the moon for you!

What to Do with Those Decluttered Friends?

So, now that you've decluttered and sorted your friends and family, you can decide the following:
- Who to keep closest to you
- Who to limit
- Who to leave

Take your Fun Acquaintances, for example. As we said earlier, they can be fun and very reliable when it comes to partying, but if you're spending too much time with them, they can start to rub off on you in a negative way. Maybe when you're in their presence, you become the "dull" person of the group, and that's not a good way to feel. They probably don't make you feel that way on purpose, but it still happens. You might want to consider heading out to party less often, or maybe with a different group of friends from time to time. You're not getting rid of your friends, but limiting your time with them.

Exes and Significant Others: Distinguishing healthy and unhealthy relationships

As a matchmaker and relationship expert, my area of specialty is recognizing compatible personalities. That is to say, individuals who share enough of the fundamentals in common that both people get their needs met. Individuals who both nurture and sustain the other in the relationship. And most of all, individuals who can co-create a relationship that is healthy, thriving, and that often leads to something long terms like marriage or a family.

Of all the relationships that you have, your most intimate relationships tend to have the most sway over your own personality makeup.

I have a colleague of mine who had been in a long-term relationship for nearly eleven years with his high school sweetheart. What had happened throughout that time was that family members would comment "she's holding you back, son ." This is a bright, ambitious individual who had achieved top marks in high school and had intended a career that involved travel, post-graduate studies, possibly even law school. His partner, however, was someone who had much more simple tastes, and she found ways to resist his impulses to go places. She would do this in different ways, sometimes deliberate, by making him feel guilty whenever he talked about traveling or insulting and berating him ("Oh, you think you're such a big shot, eh?"). Most of the time, though, her influence was unconscious.

Just by being around each other, people exchange energies in a way that isn't always equal. My colleague found that the relationship drained him over time, making him miss out on numerous opportunities when he was in his twenties and thirties.

Should you break up with your significant other if you're feeling drained? That's for you to decide, but if you do find that your relationship is dimming your light, you should ask yourself some questions.

First, how much are you giving in this relationship? My colleague did everything he could to sustain his relationship with his now-ex. He sacrificed by working jobs that were below his capabilities, living in a small apartment that met only basic needs. She, meanwhile, worked a retail job that barely paid the bills, and she relied on him for her primary income. She needed him to stay in place.

Relationships are not about keeping score, mind you, but if you feel that you're giving too much of your time, energy, or even money to your relationship than what you're getting back, it might be time for a conversation with your partner.

This isn't to say that your partner is a bad person. Sometimes, it's just a mismatch between two good people. Sometime after they had broken up, my colleague reported that his ex had met and married someone who shared many of her more simple life goals; just a simple job, a modest house, no children, and a few pets. In that regard, they were better suited for each other. My colleague, for his part, ended up finding somebody who also seemed to suit more of his needs. She was supportive of his ambitions, devoted, had some goals of her own, and was eager to make something work based on shared beliefs, shared ideas about the world, and common ground on the topics that matter, such as family and friends.

Your intimate relationships will have the most significant impact on your energy and on your ability to create. Ask yourself, does your partner dim your light? But you should also consider the flip side, are you dimming your partner's light? Are you keeping them down? Are they putting more into the relationship than what you're giving back to them?

Most of all, are you satisfied? If you're not, you both may want to consider getting to the bottom of it. Talk to a relationship counselor, a priest, rabbi, imam, or someone who you feel safe with and understands these issues. Hire a relationship coach or take a seminar together. If you end up communicating better, you'll have a more thriving relationship. You've then transformed your closest relationship into something that empowers you. You've actually decluttered each other's baggage and limiting beliefs! Remember, your partner is also in their own world, with their own limiting beliefs and perception of who you are.

On the other hand, if, having done the work, you find that you are not a match for each other, you can end the relationship and part as friends. If you decide that you want to be friends afterward, and you find an amicable way to separate, take at least three months to work on yourself with no contact with your now-ex partner. This is so that you can re-establish your own energy away from that of your partner and ensure that when you do reconnect as friends, it's the start of a new relationship and not merely continuing an old one. A new friendship, but with the added advantage of someone who understands and respects you on an intimate level and who can then offer you insights into yourself as you transform into the best version of yourself.

Sometimes, once you separate from someone and work on yourself, you may realize that you're now more compatible with that same person. Sometimes, two people have to separate, travel their own path, work on themselves, and find that they can come back together as the more magnificent versions of themselves to make the relationship work. As you can see, you have options that aren't always dreary!

Closure on Past Relationships

And what about your exes whom you don't talk to? The ones where things ended severely?

According to an article in Psychology Today, "when given closure, we can restructure our past, present, and future in a healthy way, through understanding what went wrong and reconfiguring our story accordingly."

Let's say you've had some bad blood between you and people who were your friends in the past, people who you want to reconnect with. Maybe things - fights, arguments, decisions - have happened where you simply can't put things back the way they were before, but you still want to try to make things right. I think it's good to close things right with love and integrity.

When you've decided what kind of person you want to be, when you're about to optimize all this stuff and organize your life, before all of that, you have to have a conversation with yourself and ask "what kind of relationships do I want to have? I'm not perfect, nobody's perfect, but I think I want to be a good person and no matter how hard or how bad or whatever happened, I have to take responsibility for my part in it."

If you have relationships that are not mended, you have to go back and say "Listen, I'm sorry that whatever happened. I don't want to end things on a bad note. I'm sure you had reasons for doing what you did, I'm sure I had, but at the end of the day, I appreciate you coming into my life, and I don't want to have any kind of negative feelings about our time together. For what it's worth, I'm sorry for my part in what happened between us to ruin our friendship, and I wish you nothing but goodness."

This applies to your exes as well. Maybe there was a relationship that you had, and you never called them back, and you've always felt guilty about that. Deal with that guilt and turn it around with integrity, whether it feels right or not. Just do it, because you'll feel better after. You'll have cleared those past feelings of guilt for some of the things that you think you might have done wrong, preventing them from forming new limiting beliefs in your future.

I think it's always good to clear the air, to dissolve any negative feelings that persist from those past relationships, whether you were right or wrong. The most significant part of letting go is doing it for yourself, not for anyone else. I think of it as a cleansing of negative energy. We all have issues, some bigger than others, but it's essential to be a good person in the end.

And that this act is solely for yourself, not for the people who might have hurt you. This empowers you as a person, and the empowerment comes from taking your own power back and doing the right thing for you. It will most likely get you the respect from the people you contact.

It's important to forgive people for what they've done because like you, they've also been conditioned. They react or act based on experiences for which they're probably not at fault. Maybe they haven't looked outside of their box, right? How, then, can you blame somebody for something that they're not even aware of?

Mend those relationships. Forgive them, especially if they cheated on you: that's the kind of negativity that, when you carry it for longer than necessary, sabotages all of your future intimate relationships. Forgive those people and let go of them.

It's your choice. You don't have to interact with them, or keep them in your life . Close those doors so that you have no negative energies circling you anywhere. People will admire you for having the strength to be able to do that. And that's how you build your integrity. It's more important to have people's respect versus them liking you: those are two very different things. You don't have to like someone, but if you respect them, that's what counts.

If you don't have the option of never seeing your ex again - for example, if you both have shared custody of children - I would say work things out with them. When you leave a relationship, leave it with love and integrity. Resist the temptation to put yourself to the same level as where they're at. The quicker you resolve that negative energy in your own mind, the faster you'll be able to move on with your life. If you've done absolutely everything you can, and you're letting them go with love, and you're there to support them or be an active playing partner in whatever situation that you have positively, you've done your part.

If the other person's not meeting you halfway at all, especially with child custody, then you have to start considering legal action. At that point, let a lawyer, or maybe a mediator or a counselor, deal with that person. Hopefully, they'll get to a point where they actually start looking at themselves and making positive changes, but that's ultimately on them.

If you're the one who has hurt somebody or if you've let somebody down, apologize. Apologize for your actions. Whether you're right or wrong, it's the right thing to do because everyone wins. It helps you let go, and it helps the other person move on.

And as long as you do things based on logic and integrity, those will be the right things.

Remember what I said earlier in this book, the right decisions aren't always the easy ones. Sometimes, they're the hardest ones you're going to make.

FRIENDS AND FAMILY LISTS

Closest Friends/Family: The people who love you and who you trust the most.

- ....
- ....
- ....
- ....
- ....
- ....
- ....
- ....
- ....
- ....
- ....

Acquaintances/Work Friends (e.g. people you work with/want to know better)

- ....
- ....
- ....
- ....
- ....
- ....
- ....
- ....
- ....
- ....
- ....

Abusive/Negative People (people who hurt you or make you feel small)

- ....
- ....
- ....
- ....
- ....
- ....
- ....
- ....
- ....
- ....
- ....

Regret/Pain List (e.g. people with whom you have unfinished business, who you hurt in the past, or where things happened that ended or damaged the friendship)

- ....
- ....
- ....
- ....
- ....
- ....
- ....
- ....
- ....
- ....
- ....
- ....

Chapter 5

BUILDING YOUR BODY (AND MIND)

"You don't have to be great to start … But you have to start to be great."

Now that we've taken care of your living space and created the support system you deserve within friendships and social space, and we've let go of any negative energies hounding us, we can now turn to the most important project, which is you. This is the most important and rewarding part of your life renovation, and ultimately a new beginning. You may not feel motivated at this very moment, but you will once you start the process.

Your confidence and motivation should already be getting into gear. This will get stronger every month that you get under your belt. As much as diet and fitness have to do with longevity and health, it also has a significant impact on positive mind power and self-image. Many people struggle with self-image, which can spin out into so many negative directions and outcomes. Self-image is not what you might think it is at first blush. We associate it in our society with how you look, and while that is important, your self-image is rooted in a few things that aren't immediately obvious.

Your self-image is not only determined by how you look, but also by how you have been treated. It is also deeply rooted in those limiting beliefs and experiences we encountered growing up. Emotional scars, low self-esteem, negative experiences with people and family, and relationships that are abusive all play a starring role in how we see ourselves in our skin. Learning to understand and declutter your limiting beliefs through the steps of this book, combined with a physical exercise program, will be the one-two punch in building your armor, and a new chapter in your life.

That best version of yourself that you've committed to creating will most likely challenge you, but it will be most rewarding once you get in a groove and routine. How can we appreciate the rewards of life if we do not experience the hard work to get there? The journey matters, and makes reaching the destination that much more satisfying when you get there. These are the building blocks for your inner power, self-love, and physical health and well-being, and it's rooted in the daily rituals that you create.

Finally, all of this leads to how you express yourself in the world in terms of your personal presentation. Namely, how you feel about yourself, how you feel in your clothes, how you dress, and how others perceive you in their own worlds. We'll get to all of those and more in this chapter.

Energizing Your Body

The best way, in my experience, to work on transforming your mind and self-image is to get your body into the most energized, powerful, and healthy state you can muster. As much as we think exercise is for our bodies, the reality of it truly is that this builds our minds more than anything else. Your body simply reaps the benefits of this process.

It's my firm belief that exercise is the gateway to transformation, but only if you've got an environment that supports it. In fact, this is why I've suggested that you declutter your living space before this step. From a holistic standpoint, many people go to the gym and feel great for an hour, only to come back to a cluttered home space that's filled with bad food, old clothes and objects, and reminders of your lack of integrity in other areas of your life. You can be physically fit and yet still feel as though you have no power. Whatever positive energies you had flowing from your workout are lost within a few minutes of returning to your crappy, disempowering living space. This is why I have lists and order to the steps I'm guiding you through. Once all your tasks and decluttering are done, we can dive into the most important declutter, which is your mind and body.

By starting your workouts and exercises, at this stage, you can head to the gym, come home, and still feel great because everything around you is also in order. Not only that, but it's cozy and welcoming, further adding to your high vibration.

On the flipside, if you have everything else in your life in order, but your health and well-being are not as good, you're still not going to be able to feel that powerful positive energy. If your health sucks, you're not going live long enough to enjoy it all.

Exercise is the medicine of the future today! It is the one thing that can literally pull you out of any negative space mentally and physically. It is my number one thing that ultimately gives me the foundation to sustain anything that is thrown at me. It is my personal priority in life, as it keeps me sane. It spills this power into every aspect of my life. Exercise influences mental health, longevity, reverses the aging process and optimizes your organ efficiency. I could go on and on! But this is not an overnight task. It can take six months to a year (or longer) to transform your body, depending on where you're starting from and how aggressively you want to work at building yourself towards results. This will be a critical component to create the Total Package and will need your dedication. I always say to start slow so you can get into the groove of a routine first. That way, you won't get overwhelmed and just quit.

Creating a Daily Ritual

Have you ever seen those monks and priests who live in monasteries and all of those seemingly-boring routines that they keep? They wake up, meditate or pray, eat gruel and water for breakfast, and then they spend their whole day scrubbing stone floors or copying manuscripts. Those rituals may not seem like much (how many times can you shine the same stone on the ground?) but the reason they do what they do is because it creates a habit that reinforces their spiritual duties. They're working on their beliefs and commitments. Having rituals and routines that empower you helps to build up positive energy, a sharp mind, discipline, and order to keep things flowing in life.

Most people do have a routine, but they don't think that they do. If you have a regular job, you get up at the same time every morning. You go through the same routine of getting coffee, eating the same thing for breakfast, walking the dog, then going to your job without much thought. You drive there on autopilot, sit in traffic for a bit, and before you know it, you're there. Just another humdrum day that usually ends just as blandly. Come home, walk the dog again, eat a simple dinner, watch TV for four hours, then sleep.

What these people don't realize is they have one or more rituals that reinforce that way of life. It's unconscious, and that is the key difference between what ordinary people do, and what you and I are about to create together.

What we're going to do is design a ritual that empowers your physical, mental, and spiritual health and well-being.

This ritual will help you, on top of everything else that we've done, to create and build the greatest version of you every day.

We always will have our good, bad, and even worse days during the journey of life. However, we will also have the choice of how we want to deal with it. Now that we are building your armor, you will be able to control the amount of nonsense that tries to weasel back into your space. There is only room for substance and happiness here, right? I always choose to live with the cup half full, and I always suggest incorporating something that makes you happy into your daily routine.

If you are a music person, then listen to your favorites. If you don't have a gym membership, create a little workout drill and do 3 to 5 sets first thing in the morning or time of day that's convenient. You can enjoy your morning coffee (or what have you) and reflect on the "good things" that are happening in your life, even if it seems every single thing in your life isn't right. You can give thanks for everything that has manifested in your life to this point, and everything that will grow from here on out. You can choose to meditate (just try not to fall back asleep!). You can say "good morning" to someone you care about and wish them a fantastic day. The more great stuff you give out, the more greatness you will generate for yourself.

Here are some examples of daily rituals that I have.

I usually jump on my bike first thing in the morning and do hills for 30 min with my special drink that energizes me. I am a huge music fan and always listen to energetic music as it pumps me up during my day. Every night I ask for protection

BECOMING THE TOTAL PACKAGE

for the people I love as it makes me feel like I am not alone. I also recite Psalm 23, as I've talked about in previous chapters.

How to Create Your Daily Ritual

1. Take a good look at your goals as a reminder and reinforcement of positive choices.
2. Create a mantra of your own that empowers you and supports those goals.
3. Try to incorporate one or more of the following:
   - Expressing love and gratitude (thank the Universe for guiding you towards the right choices)
   - A healthy breakfast
   - Journaling
   - Meditation and/or prayer
   - Cleaning (especially making your bed)
   - Taking one meaningful action towards a long-term goal (e.g. putting some money into a savings account for a dream vacation that you've wanted to take)
   - Pay it forward by giving someone a nice compliment during your day (one of my favorites)

Tailor this to your own personality as much or as little as you'd like. You don't need to tell anyone else about your ritual. When you do, make sure to practice it daily. If you miss a day or two, that's fine. This isn't about perfection, it's about baby steps and commitment towards greatness and happiness. It's better to adapt slowly so you can sustain your commitments realistically, versus jumping in and feeling overwhelmed.

Build your mind, discipline and transform your body

Now that we are getting into a little routine, let's get your health and body on track to a new and improved you.

Here are the steps I suggest you take to restore your mental and physical well-being.

There is so much I could share with you, I could most likely write a book on fitness and diet alone! However, here, I can only share the most essential basics. Once we get the initial fundamentals in line to get you started, we will begin the physical renovation.

Declutter Your Fridge and Shelves: The first thing you need to do is declutter your fridge. Because once you start going to the gym, sometimes people have eating habits that work against their exercise goals. Sometimes, if you're coming from a food-driven culture or if you are a foodie and love watching Anthony Bourdain or Food Network, it can be very challenging to change your habits suddenly.

It speaks to you because it helps you remember the balance that we talked about between what I can control in my life, and what is ultimately up to God and the Universe. It helps me remember that in the worst moments or biggest challenges I may face in a day, God and the Universe will take care of me. It sets up my armor to defend my dreams and my goals against all the negativity in the society of this world.

These little rituals build me up daily and kickstart my mind and body into a state of high energy output. You can create your own positive daily rituals. I'm not saying you can't enjoy what you enjoy, you can. You just have to control the quantity, consumption, and how often you have it. You take control of everything, right? You have to start slow. In my opinion, what you need to do is declutter your cupboard space and your fridge, so you are not faced with temptation. The longer you stay on top of saying no to the bad habits, the faster you build your discipline, power, and success.

Nobody's trying to take candy away from you. If you can be good 80% of the time, you deserve to have a little treat every week. I always say, during the week, stay on a program; on a Sunday (or day of your choice), go to town. Have a cheat day. Have a feast!

Get a Checkup: When was the last time you saw your doctor for something other than an emergency? Preventative care is the most effective way to create longevity in your life. After all, how can you restore integrity to your health if you don't know where the work is needed? Do a full physical exam - complete with bloodwork - and assess your current situation. This is important, because if you have any hidden medical conditions, they could get worse if you start changing your diets and ramping up your exercise. You'll want to know about them before you start your program and transformation.

Hydrate: Start drinking more water. Men and women need to drink between 2-3 L of water daily. Try getting in as much as you can first thing when you wake up. You are most dehydrated in the morning as you had nothing for hours while you slept. Water intake (especially 2L when you wake up) is also highly beneficial for weight loss and will keep you out of the bathroom at night. If you get bored with water try using fruits, cucumber, mint or berries infused in your water to help you drink more.

Cut Out Sugar: Once you've gotten an assessment from your doctor and you've started drinking your water every day, it's time to tackle your sugar intake. If you did just one thing on this list, cutting out sugar would be the most beneficial long-term decision you could make. Sugar is everywhere: in the coffee you drink, in fruits, pop, and juice. There is a huge misconception when it comes to how much sugar is in fruit. Yes, they have lots of antioxidants, but the sugar content is huge, and it's often overlooked. You don't need to be an expert to know that too much sugar is bad for you. From diabetes and heart conditions to obesity and brain fog, the consequences of a sugar-filled diet are well-known to most people. Sugar also feeds cancer cells, and has a overall negative impact on our health and bodies. As I said before, this isn't to say you can't have dessert from time to time, but make sure that whatever sugar you take in is heavily-restricted and saved only as a treat or in moderation.

No Meals at Night: Once you have the first three steps in control and you're ready for the next decision, stop having meals after 8 o'clock at night as best you can. Among other things, this will help you sleep better (notice how late-night snacks tend to keep you awake). Sleep is one of the most important factors when it comes to optimal daily performance and vitality. A lot of us take sleep for granted, especially those who say "I'll sleep when I'm dead." And yes, I get it, but do not underestimate the importance of sleep and how it affects your mood, concentration, focus, performance, skills, and the list goes on. Do what you can, and remember practice makes perfect.

Energize Your Metabolism: From here on out, we're going to crank your metabolism to the heavens in the two most basic ways you can imagine: diet and exercise.

Diet: Let's say that, during that first month, you eliminate all sugar, drink enough water, and stop eating late. Do that for awhile until it becomes systematic and easy. We want to make sure that we break you into this new habit slowly. If you do it too fast, you might overwhelm yourself and your lizard brain will just shut everything down.

Exercise, Part I: Start to lightly exercise your body every day for even just 15 minutes at a time. Whether it's a quick jog around the block from your front door or spending an hour on a treadmill or elliptical at the gym, cardio will energize your body which will, in turn, energize every other aspect of your being. Personally, I prefer running on a track or treadmill. I jog or cycle every day, not only for exercise, but to help me get my mind into high vibration. It's also my backup plan whenever I feel down or have had a long, stressful day. For now, you don't have to do anything intense, but make sure to start getting used to moving your body every day. You can follow my timeline or create your own based on your schedule. However, you need to be committed and consistent to get the results to change your mind and body.

Starting on your second month, keep your meals small, whatever they may be. I don't believe in one diet or another because things work differently for different people, but just having good eating habits in general. That's what I'm helping you build for yourself, however it may look for you. In fact, make sure to have smaller meals more often during the day. There are definitely some great guidelines that are available for you if you do the research.

Do all of these things together, and you'll be feeling wonderful in no time! You'll find it easier to wake up in the morning. Brain fog that usually hangs around disappears. Your urge to snack goes away as your blood and glycemic levels balance out.

Yes, you might have thyroid issues or other health complications which will impact how much you can do and the way you do it when it comes to your food and exercise. If those are your reasons for being overweight, for example, that's perfectly understandable and you should follow your doctor's advice on how to manage them.

However, for many people, bad health, weight gain, and obesity are the result of bad eating habits. Many of them have been instilled in us by our parents, and if you're not careful, how you ate at home as a kid determines how you eat on your own as a grown-up. It's why in the United States, the biggest killer is obesity. Because your organs can't handle the weight, they start to deteriorate, and since you actually have no clue what's happening on the inside of your body, you'd never feel anything until really late in the game. It's like in the show *Dr. Oz*, when they test how old you really are. You might look like you're in your thirties or forties on the outside, but you're actually 60 years old on the inside based on how you eat and how you treat your body. If you learn that self-respect and self-love, you're going to only want to put the right things in your body. Not only are you going to feel better, but you're going to perform better and you're going to look better! Now would be a good time to consult with a nutritionist or a dietician or a personal trainer as we are all very well equipped in steering you in the right direction with the support you need. You can also pick up a book and educate yourself on the topic, but here are some important guidelines I can share with you.

1. Eat 3 small meals a day and 3 snacks.
2. Eat every 3 hours to speed up metabolism and reduce hunger pains or cravings.
3. Eat lots of dark green veggies like broccoli, spinach, green beans, kale etc. with every meal except for snacks.
4. Eat enough protein daily for your body weight.
5. Incorporate healthy fats into every meal such as avocado, flaxseed, or your healthy preference.
6. Eat healthy carbs like yams, brown rice, or quinoa, preferably for lunch. Dinner should always be your lightest meal.

7. Stay away from fruits especially at night. Yes, they are healthy, and they have lots of antioxidants, but they are very high in sugar. If you are consuming fruits, at least have them in the morning so you can burn it during the day. Fruits that are lower in sugar include apples, pears, grapefruits, and berries such as raspberries, strawberries, and blueberries.
8. Try to keep your alcohol consumption to a minimum as it is very high in sugar and will impact your performance. Alcohol can also influence you as a depressant when your mental energy is low.
9. Try to scale down or eliminate your dairy consumption, as it has an impact on your hormone levels, skin, and bloating.
10. Make sure to take a good multivitamin for your age group, fish oils, or omega 3s. Ladies might appreciate a strong biotin or silica vitamin to help with your hair and nails. Also, if you feel like you are always tired with no energy or lethargic, or maybe losing your hair, check your iron as you may need to incorporate it into your supplements.

These are just basic examples of what works. Not only are you going to feel better, but you're going to perform better, and you're going to look better! There is overwhelming science that backs this up that you can research on your own time.

Your eating is one of the hardest habits to transform. How can you not eat everything you've gotten used to eating, right? It's very hard to retrain your habits, but you can get to a point where you're actually craving the good stuff. Hang in there long enough, and you're going to start seeing some surprising changes. One day, you'll begin to crave salads the way that you used to crave pizza. You may find that your taste buds completely change.

The secret is to think of food as a fuel source, and your body as a sports car that needs premium, high octane gas at all times!

Exercise, Part II: After a month of creating new eating habits and getting your body used to the change, it's time to ramp up that bit of daily exercise into full-blown training! When you do this, you're going to see your health and weight loss results double in a short period of time. Start a physical training program maybe twice a week. If you can afford a trainer, hire a trainer to keep you accountable and guarantee the results you want. If you're going to work out on your own, look for videos on YouTube or other routines that work for you. Your training could involve anything from workouts at a gym, Zumba, maybe even a martial art like boxing, taekwondo, aikido, or krav maga. Whatever works for you, do that for at least one hour a day if you can.

As long as you have your food and nutrition under control, and as long as you're sticking to the routine 80 percent of the time, you're going to get the results that you want.

Don't just look at your reflection in the mirror and guess that everything's working: take measurements. The most important thing if you're trying to lose weight is that you're shrinking in inches and not just pounds. You might not see ten, twenty, or thirty pounds coming off in the first month, but you'll most likely notice your body starting to change. The results vary from person to person. And remember, muscle weighs more than fat, so don't freak out if you are losing more inches than pounds.

Now, to be clear, you don't need to look like Schwarzenegger or Gisele Bundchen to feel amazing. Really, you can be any body type and be attractive and energized. What counts is that you feel comfortable and confident in your own skin. How you look might not be as important as how you feel.

And don't forget to invite your close friends - the ones we identified in the last chapter - to join you. If you can't afford your own personal trainer but still want that kind of support and accountability, having a close friend join you at the gym will not only give you those things but also allow your friend to work on their own health and fitness.

What kind of training should you do? This depends on your physical ability at the time, your health history, and what you are trying to achieve with your goals. It's much more effective to do something high intensity. But it also depends on what kind of results you want. If you want endurance, if you want a strong cardiovascular system, if you want to be stronger, faster, leaner, or stockier, you might need to try different routines to find the best fit for you.

Whatever you pick, aim to stick to it at least 80% of the time. All of this builds your discipline. It's rewarding, not just for its own sake, but because you're accomplishing something. And just knowing that you're achieving a major goal is enormous for the mind. Exercise gives you endorphins, motivates you to do more, build more, and feel more, on every level. If you're going through a bad relationship breakup, if you are stressed in your working life, the best thing you can do is get into the gym and just start sweating it out. The worst thing that will come of that is that you will have less stress, and you'll feel better physically and mentally. To me, exercise should be your go-to, your number one recipe for any kind of pain or struggle that you feel. It's a great outlet, and it keeps your mind sane.

If, at any moment you're feeling a little bit low and you want to recharge, go for a brisk walk. If you want to do more, run. Running is probably the number one thing that will de-stress your mind and your body. Somebody might find cycling to be their thing, somebody else might like racquetball, but for me personally, it's running. If you can't run right away, take baby steps. Go for a brisk walk and then start and stop. Maybe run one lap and walk the next. Whatever you can do is good enough, but as long as you have the strength or the power to get yourself out of the house and do something, I guarantee you're going to feel better by the time you get back.

What all of this does is feed your longevity and change the energy that you emit into the world that others see? The longer you stick with it, the more you're going to discover your ability to overcome your limits, and the better you're going feel. You're going to see the body change in front of you, and you won't ever want to go back!

Best yet, all of this feeds into the next cycle of your new and exciting chapter of life. When you walk out the door, more people are going to notice you, not only because of how you look but by the light that you seem to shine on everything around you, a light that comes from the confidence and pride of having made a change and accomplishing your goals.

As you've created your space, managed your relationships, restored your body to health and wellness, and created daily empowering rituals, the Universe will send you opportunities and great experiences.

Feeling Good, Looking Good: Fashion and Wardrobe

Now that you are feeling and looking better, it's time to move on to the next part of the plan . And as I've said in previous chapters, if you want to get your head right, you need to get your threads right. How do we do that?

When was the last time you went shopping for clothes? If you'll recall during your decluttering chapter, you went through your closets and drawers and got rid of anything that you hadn't worn in the last six months. Anything non-essential that you were just keeping around for no good reason. Now we're going to go about and replace your wardrobe and re-create it in a way that reflects the brilliant new "you" that we have been working on this entire book so far.

So, how do you want the world to see you? Where can you get some ideas?

Why do we do this? Your self-image is just as important as this also connects to how you relate to the people in your life. Obviously, having just decluttered your friends and managed your relationships in an empowering way, we know that the people around you won't judge you for what you wear (or at least won't judge you harshly if you have a casual day). However, if you've ever walked into a room looking and feeling great, you know the power that you command in those moments. You've felt it. This is what we're going to create on an everyday basis in your self-image. It's not about just what you project to others, but the feeling of power that you experience. You want others to see you, in their worlds, as a confident, powerful, positive person filled with energy who they want to be around, and who's going to add that joy and light to the world. You can do that through the power of clothes.

First of all, look to your mentors. Everyone starts off by imitating what they know, so look to the people who inspire you in movies or TV, or even within your close friends. Look at how they present themselves. The odds are pretty good that they're not sloppy in any way much of the time. This isn't to say that you need to be a clothes horse or a fashionista. There's no need to be superficial, there are many perfectly reasonable people who wear sloppy jeans and old shoes, no makeup, hair in a ponytail, etc. You can wear anything you want without diminishing your value as a person. Your clothes don't represent your worth as a human being, but they can serve as a projection of your best self when you want them to.

Look at your heroes or your she-roes and see how they dress. Where do they shop? This isn't necessarily about the brand names, this is about what the outfit looks like. What is the image that you want to project? Look through catalogs and the internet. Save some pictures, then print them out in color and look at them daily. Then, when you have a clear idea, go shopping.

You can find really great clothes anywhere you want. However, consider that the high-end stores are high-end for a reason. The brand names and high-fashion labels also tend to make high-quality clothing that lasts. Go window shopping at first, then go try them on.

You'll want to look for clothes that feel good - not just flatter your form, but help you feel confident, empowered, all of those qualities that we've been building - and of course look good. Bring one of your most trusted friends with you who knows you best, and who is honest to give you positive, constructive feedback. Also, there are plenty of extraordinary image consultants who can guide you and truly help you identify your personal style. I am happy to share some of their wisdom with you here and will provide excellent references at the end of this book.

Everything is Connected

All right, let's take a breath!

From the very start of this book, we've renovated nearly every aspect of your life, but as I said in the introduction, I believe in a holistic approach to living your best life. Now that you've reached this point, I want to show you how it all connects.

First, you envisioned your desires and wrote them down in detail. This triggered the Law of Attraction to start working for you, as well as helping you identify your goals and dreams.

Next, you transformed your living space, getting rid of old junk and re-creating it in a way that it sustains positive energy and makes you feel good to come home. It's cozy and comfortable and makes you feel oh so good!

You then managed your relationships and made sure to surround yourself with the people who supported your best self at any given moment.

Following that, you transformed your self-image through a daily ritual, healthy eating, and exercise, then wearing new clothes that showed the best part of you to others.

If you've done all those things, I want you to take a look at your life as you're now living it.

Let's say you've come home from a great, sweaty workout at the gym, a little sore but feeling pumped and positive! Your living room - tidy, organized, and decorated in a way that reflects your personality and energy - welcomes you, makes you feel good to be home. You decide to invite some of your close friends over for a healthy dinner, friends who you know will make for great company because you're spending more time with the ones who believe in you. A few hours later, your friends come over, and immediately you feel even more positive energy in your life. You're cooking, eating, drinking, and laughing all night long, and by the time you all decide to call it a night, hours have gone past, and it feels like it just flew by, you were having so much fun! You then turn in for bed, maybe performing a daily meditation ritual, giving thanks to the Universe for a beautiful day, before falling into a deep, restful sleep.

It all connects, and what's more, huge things are going to start happening very soon!

People are going to feel that light around you, and they'll want to be part of that light because that's how human beings are. Why do you think people want to hang around with people who are outgoing, funny, fun, and happy? Because it affects them. They become comfortable and fun around those people, so they always want to be around that energy.

And, if you've done all this and you're single, intending to meet the person of your dreams, you can guess what will happen next...

Chapter 6

GETTING BACK IN THE (DATING) GAME

"To know when to go away and when to come closer is the key to any lasting relationship."

B y now, some interesting things should be happening to you when you walk into a room.

Whether it's a casual party or a fancy restaurant, I'm always looking around the room. I entertain myself with observing people, and I can look at someone and see how they dress and how they carry themselves and pretty much know what kind of life they have. What their personality could be like.

The ones who get my attention just seem to have a light around them. They're not necessarily the prettiest or most handsome, not always dressed in fancy, formal clothes, but they radiate powerful positive energy everywhere they go. Heads turn when they walk into the room. Everyone just wants to go talk to them. By just being around, they command attention.

If you've done everything I've told you to do in this book so far, you've no doubt turned your share of heads everywhere you've gone. That's the confidence that comes with having everything all together.

And, sooner or later, you're going to attract a different kind of attention, the kind that could change your life forever. Namely, the partner of your dreams.

For many of you, this is the part of the book you've been waiting for the most.

As I talked about way back at the start of our journey together, the best way to go about attracting your soulmate is to become the kind of person who your soulmate would want to be with. In this way, you'll make it much easier for them to know you when they see you.

Even if you're already in a happy relationship, I will encourage you to read this chapter anyway. We're going to talk about some principles of being the right partner that can only benefit what you've already got with your significant other.

But if the reason you've become the Total Package is to find that special someone, this chapter will show you how to put that new glow that you carry with you to good use. Of course, it probably won't be as easy as just walking into the room and having all kinds of people come up to you, but then again, who's to say what the Universe has in store for you?

I'm going to show you how to be the right person, at the right place, at the right time, for when the future love of your life steps into the room. You remember when you first started this journey, you thought someone else, a new relationship, was going to be the thing that pulled you out of the water? Look at how different you are. Do you still feel that way?

If you start dating again, you're going to have a lot of those old limiting beliefs and heartbreaks pop up again. This is natural, and when that happens, watch for them. I've shown you how to deal with them.

Dating as the Total Package

As I've said throughout this book, a person who is the Total Package knows how to make the right decisions and is emotionally-sound. Meaning that now that you've conditioned yourself, and been through the journey, you've learned how to deal with the negative positively. You've learned how to make better choices for yourself. Whether it's business, romantic, or what have you, the way that you deal with people in any relationship will be very different than before because no one can affect you now. You are in control of yourself. Someone could argue with you, but you don't let it touch you as much, because you understand the nature of limiting beliefs and that it has nothing to do with you personally. Your actions and reactions will be different than they were before.

Through this transformation and knowledge, you're able to dictate the kind of life you want to have. That makes you the Total Package because you will not be influenced by negative things as easily. You know how to deal with them, which creates a very safe ground for building relationships. People can see that you don't react. People will sense all this goodness around you! You have emotional stability and high emotional IQ. Now you think things through differently, a little bit more logically. This is all super fulfilling stuff! Not only are you in great shape and look good when you meet someone, but that person is also going to want to be with you. They've seen what's out there, and all of a sudden, there's someone here who sees the world differently, in a positive way. Not only do you look incredible on the outside, you now have more substance and integrity to offer anyone that you choose to have in your life. This is the energy you're putting out.

Attraction in dating isn't always logical. You can walk into a room, see the most gorgeous person there and have a conversation with them, and there's nothing but self-doubt, negative energy, inexperience, or some aspect where you think, "um, no, what's on the outside doesn't match what's on the inside." And then you have a person who walks into a room and maybe they look a little more average, but they're smart, they understand how the world works, and they really bring something great to the table in terms of their emotional stability and point of view, they have the right kind of perception. These are people who don't just react but think things through because they understand the world better. They have a choice in how they deal with things. That's very attractive to others.

Expectations and Assumptions

Remember earlier chapters when I told you that you are in control of your destiny? That everything happens for a reason? And anything is possible? Now that you have taken control of your life, and have been building a healthy foundation, you will be able to enjoy your life on a whole new level, and this will allow you to create great new relationships and opportunities. I would like you to remember that people come into our lives for a reason, a season, or a lifetime, and there is no reason not to enjoy every aspect of all three. Everything is an experience that will bring you either knowledge, a lesson, a great time, growth as an individual, or the love of your life when meeting new people on your journey. Welcome, this possibility with open arms. You are now living in integrity with more understanding and knowledge of self, and this will pave a road filled with great experiences, substance, and happiness that no one can ever take away from you.

One of the biggest mistakes that people unconsciously make is having expectations and assumptions around their situations with people. This is how we set ourselves up for many disappointments. It's quite simple: if we don't have the expectations, we are less likely to be disappointed, right? All we can do is control how we respond and act towards people and what we choose to give. When it comes to people, all we need to do is pay attention to how they respond and treat us, as we are now able to see the nonsense and identify the behaviors that come with limited beliefs in others. I always say that no matter who comes into your life, time will tell you everything you need to know about them.

The attraction is where most people have a lot of false expectations. Men and women are quite different, and they also have plenty of unrealistic expectations when it comes to dating or relationships. For example, men tend to be very visual. Initially, the Total Package in a woman, to a typical man, is very much rooted in how they look and their style. Once they start getting to know you, they will decide if you are the marrying type or the fun type. In this example, the question is whether you've come into their life for a season, or a reason, or a lifetime? Women ask the same question, though they tend to evaluate men based on their personality and character than their appearance (though, of course, he should look and smell good on the date). Is he funny? Is he smart? Is he kind?

All are okay as long as there are no expectations or assumptions, and both parties are honest about what they are looking for. There are all kinds of relationships out there, and none of them deserve judgment as people are entitled to live their lives in a way that makes them happy. They can have an open relationship or swing with others. They can be bisexual. They can enjoy bondage or any other means of pleasure they desire. What people decide they want within their personal relationships with each other is their choice. We all have our preferences in what turns us on and what doesn't, and in my opinion, everything is okay as long as it makes everyone involved happy. You just need to know and understand yourself and choose your happiness path when you make the right connection. The same way we compartmentalized our relationships and friendships in the decluttering chapter, is the same way we choose how we want to share our time in new relationships. Now that we know what we want our life to be like in the decisions we have made until this point, this sets you up as the Total Package to be ready to attract the same. Over time you will be able to see things in people more quickly and decide if they are someone you want in your life, so be patient.

There are so many possibilities when it comes to an attraction that if you're reacting based on looks alone, you could get into trouble because you don't know what's on the inside. Or, if your expectations are too high, you're going to find mistakes no matter who you meet.

Now that you have your armor, try to be totally open and accepting towards others as you never know how they can surprise you. We have a fantasy about the kind of person we want to meet; we build up this expectation in our heads, and we ignore or let go of other people who don't meet this vision. But if you stop long enough to meet someone different and get to know them on the inside, you might be surprised at who you'll find. As long as you know the important things that you want, figure out what those are, and then make your secondary list of items where you're willing to compromise. As long as you know what those are, the right person will present themselves to you sooner or later. And if you've done the work on yourself, your perspective on dating will have also changed. You'll see that sometimes the goodness in another person comes in a different package than what you've set yourself up to expect.

Never have any expectations, assumptions, or reactions when it comes to the dating game. Let people show you what you need to see. Be open to possibilities. If someone, say, wants to introduce you to someone else, find out some details. Are their parents still together? How were they raised? You might not need to ask these questions on a first date, but if you feel really great and confident energy from them, you should be able to ask these kinds of personal questions with ease and have them respond in kind. What is your lifestyle like? Do you travel? What are your favorite things to do? Things you like? Most healthy minded people tend to appreciate a more direct approach when getting to know someone. It shows confidence and a no-nonsense approach in knowing what you want, and this is very attractive to other confident candidates.

You're asking this information not necessarily to fit an expectation, but because this is the first step in experiencing this person as they are. When you meet somebody, it doesn't matter what happens in the beginning, time is going to tell you everything. I would also advise you not to make any big decisions and don't jump into things. You don't know what's inside that person until you both get a little bit more comfortable with each other, and you allow yourselves to be more vulnerable in the relationship. Sometimes, too, people will show you who they are in their actions. Not everyone is always themselves at the very beginning, they are usually a little on guard to start off.

For someone part of a younger generation that has known things like "friends with benefits" and other blurred lines around dating, you will want to be direct with them and what they are looking for. Something serious? Or something fun? If you know what you want, you should make sure that you're not spending your time and energy on someone who has a different desire in mind. If the person says that they aren't sure, wait and see. After a couple of months of dating each other, you should have the conversation around being exclusive, and then you'll know exactly where things will go at that point. If you do find it's taking too long, don't hesitate to press the other person to have the talk. Sit down with them and convey to them, as honestly and as positively as possible "I like you, and I don't want to play any games. I'd like to know where you want to take what we're doing." It shows a level of integrity and respect, and if your partner is the right person, they'll respect it.

There are so many things I could say about dating and relationships, I could write another book! But for now, I'll stick to the essential elements.

Gender and Orientation

Before we continue, I want to touch on something. In today's world, where the conversations around gender are different than they've been in the past, if you don't identify as "man" or "woman" or if you're not heterosexual, the same principles apply. The same gestures, commitments, work, and responsibilities to learn about each other applies. It's more about the "masculine" or "feminine" energies than the actual identity, and it applies no matter your sexual orientation. However the energies mix for you in your body, find a partner who will meet your needs and nurture you in the same way.

No matter how you identify yourself, communication is universal, as is always doing the right thing and treating each other with respect. Your commitment to the person and your expression of The Total Package applies no matter your gender, so as you continue to read this book, wherever you hear me mention "men" or "women," think "masculine" or "feminine" energy. I use the terms for the ease of my communication, with no disrespect or intention to disappear any particular person or group of people.

Differences Between Men and Women

Not only are men and women very different, but there are various subcategories within each man or woman. There's "passive", "passive-aggressive", "alpha males," "introverts/extroverts", and so on. It's very tough to find your way in relationships. You don't always know what you're getting.

A lot of the time, though, when you learn or understand what a man's needs or a woman's needs are, it's easier to work that within relationships. You'll have to know exactly what you're there to do in the relationship. It comes with the territory.

Men and women alike are emotional. The way they show emotion is often different, and of course, there are different scales of that. You can meet an emotional man, but only shows it in one way. He might offer you gifts, or spend time with you, or offer words of validation to you, and so on. Women are socialized to talk about their emotions from a very young age. Where it's not encouraged in men, it's expected of women, so it makes sense that women will need more in the way of communication about their feelings.

Women like to feel that feminine energy, and the more we feel that energy, the more we want to share it with our men. That's how many of us are wired. From the moment we stand in front of the mirror to when we walk out the door, to when we enter a room full of people, we carry that energy everywhere with us. But it's possible to lose that energy within relationships without encouragement.

Men and women need to understand that when they are in a relationship that the honeymoon isn't the whole thing. This is actually a contract. To a certain degree, every relationship is a job, with specific job requirements. For men, for example, it's vital that the man in the relationship feels that his partner is supportive of what he's doing. And for women, typically, it's crucial to feel that she has been seen and heard by her partner. Of course, these are generalizations: every couple is different, and each partner has their own unique needs and wants as individuals. In any case, the relationship requires upkeep, attention, and care from both partners to make it work in the way it's supposed to.

For example, men like to be nurtured as well. I am talking about being nurtured emotionally and sexually, whether it's you making them dinner, giving them a shoulder massage when they come home, or those sweet little things that we do for our partners that we sometimes don't feel like doing. That's what I mean when I say it's like a job: you might be tired, but if you know your partner enjoys it, you should do it. They don't call it "emotional labor" for nothing!

This is especially true of men. The way that men are socialized is very different from how women are socialized. If you're a straight, North American dude, you have a touch deficit. Men tend not to hug, so they're missing that sense of physicality. That also has to do with how they were brought up by their parents: some people were more touch-driven, others were more distant. Women, on the other hand, are expected to be comfortable with touch from a young age, regardless of their upbringing. It's taken for granted that women like to touch and be touched more than men, whether it's true or not.

The bottom line: women need to feel very good about themselves. If we don't have that sense of well-being and just feeling attractive, we won't have it in us to give back to you. Women tend to shut down in that respect within a relationship. Their partners will start noticing that they've gone quiet, never seem happy, and often, they won't recognize that it stems from a lack of being made to feel beautiful.

Men, for their part, are the same way. When they're not getting their needs met, they may get distant. They'll start looking for that sense of fun and validation somewhere else, not necessarily in another woman, but maybe a golf game, a bar, or some other activity that takes him away from you.

Vulnerability in Relationships

Now, after reading those last two paragraphs, some of you may be thinking "wasn't the whole point of becoming the Total Package so that we wouldn't need a partner to feel our own power and attractiveness?" This might seem like a contradiction, but when you dig a little deeper, you'll find that it makes sense. It all has less to do with validation, which is what a great life gives you, and more to do with vulnerability when you share that life with someone else.

Being the Total Package means taking responsibility. It does mean renovating your life in all of its aspects, as we've done – your living space, your health, your friends, your personal presentation, and so on – such that, even without a romantic partner, you can be happy with your life.

When you enter into a relationship, however, you start to find yourself needing more, like having a safe space to feel vulnerable, or someone to talk to when you're feeling low down. Being the Total Package doesn't mean every day is going to be perfect. You're still going to have bad days, days when things are not going your way, or when something's happened to take the wind out of your sails. When that happens, who are you going to turn to for support? Yes, you've got your closest friends, but if you're in a relationship, you're most likely going to go to your partner first.

When you enter into a relationship, it's now not only about you, it's about both of you. New needs and desires will open up that you didn't think that you had and that you probably wouldn't have had when you were single. Just as limiting beliefs will start coming up for you, they'll also begin to come up for your partner. It's up to the both of you to co-create a safe, loving space where you both can let your guards down and meet each other's needs (such as being listened to, being reminded of your beauty, being respected for what you do, etc .). And, should you both decide to break up, you'll still have the life that you built for yourself. You should never lose yourself in a relationship, but neither should you hold back from being open and vulnerable when you're in one.

That's the balancing act. On your own, you are independent. Within a relationship, you become a little bit interdependent, and that's perfectly fine.

For relationships, once you understand your partner's needs, you need to look after them every day, and they need to do the same for you. That's what keeps the relationships bonded and committed.

If you're the Total Package, you know that there's a certain way that your energy feels when you're taking action from that place. When you know you're doing the right things if you've been doing so since the beginning to attract your partner, why wouldn't you keep doing it once you're in the relationship?

Lastly, always remember that the specific wants and needs of each partner will depend on the partner. These are just general guidelines that I've seen in the men and women I've worked with.

Trust

The more negative experiences we have with people, the more they condition us to have less trust and confidence. They cause us to lose faith. When someone beats you over the head enough times, you're going to start to believe that you deserve it. When you break up with someone, or if you're dating people and they all seem to be without integrity, just playing games with you and disappointing you, it's understandable. Because we're good, we automatically assume they're going to be good. That's how we are and is a basic expectation of other people, but that's not how it is.

When I raise my children, I try to teach them to be cautious from the get-go. I planted a seed for them. There are good people who we know. There are bad people who we know (bank robbers, molesters, abusers, etc.) But there are also the "ugly."

"Ugly" people are those who pretend to be genuine, and they're not. They're deceitful, and those people I regard as wolves in sheep's clothing. You trust the sheep, you can recognize the wolves pretty quickly, but the wolves in sheep's clothing are deadly because you never see them coming. That's when it can really hit you hard.

The wolves in sheep's clothing give themselves away in subtle ways that, if you are clear about yourself and fully awake, you can tell via your intuition. Go by your gut feeling, it's the best compass that you have. Sure, you can be wrong sometimes, but it's still overall the most reliable way to go. Those people can be devastating to your sense of trust.

If the reason why you picked up this book is because someone broke your heart, that's one of the worst breaches of trust, even if they did nothing wrong. This is partly what makes it ugly. It's the person who you woke up next to every day, who you trusted not to hurt you emotionally or physically, and although they didn't do anything out of sorts, you still feel as though *they* ripped your heart out. It's only natural, and it's only natural afterward to have your sense of trust broken. This is why it's essential, to be honest with each other. Being brutally honest is more respectful than holding back, versus someone really nice and amazing, but they're just stirring up the pot behind the scenes. Which would you prefer? Would you prefer the brutally honest truth or someone who's pulled the wool over your eyes, making you feel that everything is okay, only to turn around and smash your life?

Because you don't see them coming, or you may have had a very recent experience of someone doing that to you, when you do see other people, you no longer know how to identify the sheep from the wolves. That's why you no longer trust.

As much as you're trying to re-condition all of your limiting beliefs, you will still have those fears coming up, but having done this work, you now get to choose the positive things that you can be conditioned by. This now becomes your choice. This is why those right decisions are so important. This is part of building your armor, so you can do better next time. That's how you can learn from your mistakes and from people. This is the best way to understand them.

When people become negative from their negative experiences, it's tough to work past that. The more you keep that negativity close to you, the more you're going to make choices and engage in behaviors that will reinforce negativity. You'll create reasons as to why you won't commit to someone interested in you or make other excuses for why you can't trust that person. You'll be afraid to put yourself in specific environments because you'll be fearful of having the same incident happen again. Still, by keeping the negative way, you're also keeping the positive away. There's no way to keep out one and let in the other. The best way to learn how to identify that negativity is to do the work on yourself and become more self-aware so that you can discern the behavior in other people and tell the sheep from the wolves in sheep's clothing.

And it takes time. I didn't get here in a year or a month, but it took decades of this kind of work. It takes time, but you grow into someone who can tell the difference.

Hurt People Can Hurt People

Being the Total Package in your own life gives you that kind of insight into other people. You can trust yourself to identify the good, the bad, and the ugly. That's because being the Total Package isn't just about having a nice-looking body, your hair in order, your nails done, or being well-dressed. There are a lot of people out there with all those things, but they're not the whole package. For those people, what the outside is portraying is very different from what's on the inside. They're surface people, looking really good, but in disarray on the inside. They've likely had negative experiences. Maybe they have commitment issues because someone broke their hearts or took a lot of money from them in a divorce. That's a big deal. And yet, they look like the total package, but now with all of this heartbreak.

If you dwell on the negativity too long, you're in great danger of becoming ugly. If you choose to have fun rather than look for a serious relationship, but you still haven't healed your past experiences and limiting beliefs, you're very likely to learn how to say and do the right things to bring in someone who is looking to you for a long-term commitment that you have no intention of delivering. You want to know where ugly people come from. They were hurt in a very similar way to how you were, but they made different choices. They gave up. They decided this was all life wanted for them, that "if you can't beat them, join them," and that's not the right answer. Simply, they are very lost.

If you're reading this, I'm assuming you don't want to become that. Understand, though, in the worlds of ugly people, that's how it works. You are genuine, but you are in danger of becoming ugly, the longer you dwell in negativity. That's why we're doing this work.

That's why it's also imperative to have faith. When you have faith in a higher power to help you with that responsibility of staying authentic and genuine in a scary world, that's what will guide you. Even if you don't have anything already in the world that you can believe in that way, if you create it for yourself, you'll see that there is goodness there. And the goodness really is there, many beautiful people in the world are just as beautiful as you are.

If you can't find trust, you create it, the same way that you can create goodness. In order to create trust, you need to have the courage to be the first one to trust. The majority of connections happen between two right partners when one of them takes that risk, to allow themselves to be vulnerable. The important thing is to know yourself. So you'll see that you're vulnerable, that you're going through things, and that you're scared. There is a lot of fear around this subject, but to know that you are making the decision to be strong despite all of these things is powerful. That's really all you need. And that power is going to grow inside of you. The ability to know that you decided to be the person that, despite all odds and the negatives, you wanted to be stronger than all of those things trying to pull you down. To be better.

When you decide that, even with all of the risks that come with going against the grain, you'll be rewarded in so many ways - because that's when you connect with the right people. Vulnerability is the one common thread that connects good people.

It's okay if you get hurt. Pain is part of life, but you just need to know how to deal with it, so it doesn't turn into long-term negativity. Make the right decisions with courage, and you'll get to wherever you want to be.

Are you that person? No? Then become that person!

Chivalry: Very Much Alive

Chivalry is definitely not dead when it comes to relationships. I think courage is a natural human sentiment and action that people will respond to. You treat people with goodness, they'll want to give goodness back. If you take that way, what do you have?

Chivalry can take you back to how men and women are. It's not just about holding doors. It's about making your partner feel attractive, about making them feel confident and supported, through your actions. It's about those little things that matter because they all add up to build a person. There are still chivalrous people out there, but as technology has broken down these values in the younger generations, it's increasingly hard to find such people. Just as you as a parent will model behaviors for your kids by showing them what a loving relationship looks like, the technology that you give them access to will start to affect their viewpoints. It's important to limit or regulate the use of their technology and teach them the proper context of what they're seeing. You can model chivalry for your kids as well.

Chivalry isn't hard. I had a client once who sent flowers to his date before the date. "I just wanted to put a smile on your face," he said to her. And it worked! Other gestures are what we'd expect: hold their bag, open the door for them, pick up the bill. You're not doing these things because you're trying to imply that they are less capable, but to show them that you want to take care of them. After all, they've spent most of the week opening their own doors, paying for things, cooking, having to carry around all their stuff on their own. Anyone would welcome the break that you offer through chivalrous actions like these. It will make them feel like an epiphany. And what does that make them want to do, over time? Take you home and jump your bones! Everybody wants to be taken care of men and women. That's what chivalry should be, helping other people feel taken care of.

Testing Your Confidence and The Truth About Rejection

Confidence is attractive. Men and women love confident people. Throughout this book, you've been working on your self-image too, among other things, build up your confidence. But you have to see that confidence through! That is, you need to test it. One of the top fears that almost every person has about approaching someone to whom they are potentially attracted is fear of rejection. It's right up there with fear of public speaking and spiders.

Let's say you meet somebody who you're interested in asking out. Up until this point, you've been rocking it on your own with your rituals, your fitness and nutrition, your new threads, and your empowering digs. You're on top of the world! And then you find out that some of those old voices in your brain that you thought had gone away - your limiting beliefs - are still around. "Oh, I'm going to get rejected" or "they're going to think I'm an idiot," and this and that. Suddenly, they come roaring back, and you lose your nerve.

Remember, when two people are meeting, each person is in their own box of experiences, preferences, and perspectives. Not everyone likes the same people. Everyone has been conditioned to a high degree by their environment and the lives they've led. As a result, they will react to you differently than they would to someone else. What that means is that who you are has almost nothing to do with how they treat you! It's all about their perception, meaning if they reject you, it's nothing personal. (Sometimes, when people say "it's not you, it's me," they really mean it!)

Also, consider that you have been conditioned a certain way to think and feel that rejection can actually hurt you. Again, this is based on your own experiences (maybe you asked out the prom queen or king in high school and got shot down, or maybe you had a critical parent or teacher). You might think that when someone says "I'm not interested", it's an invalidation. Most of the time, though, it isn't. The other person is simply not interested for their own reasons.

If you look at it that way, that means no rejection is personal. It also means that you don't need to be afraid of rejection. Finally, it means that you can not only be yourself around someone new who's caught your eye, but you can talk to them and ask them out without fear. In life, you will meet a lot of people for a lot of different reasons. Look at it as opportunities for creating new friendships, or business and networking opportunities, or meeting a love interest. It's really all about the energy that we carry inside. This energy seeks someone with that same energy, and when you meet that person, and you feel that strong chemistry or connection without being able to explain it, that is what I am talking about. The physical attraction is just the initial superficial level of connection, but when you feel someone or connect mentally or emotionally, that is the real deal kind of energy.

On the other hand, if you have somebody who's a happy person, who's got a little bit of confidence, that's had more positive experiences in their life versus negative, who appreciates and loves themselves first, those qualities will shine through as you make your first contact.

Eye Contact

This is another big mistake that I see people making, especially people 35 and under. Eye contact equals confidence. When you can look another human being in the eye, you demonstrate that you are honest, courageous, and confident.

Smiling

Smile at people. You'd be surprised at what happens. Smile at people everywhere without any expectation of anyone smiling back. When you're building your confidence, and you're working out, and you're doing things for yourself, test the water.

In the worlds of the other people, you now show up as this happy person who stands out, possibly even someone they want to get to know better.

Don't underestimate the power of this simple act of human connection. A friend of mine was once sitting on a bench in a park, feeling down on himself, when a stranger walked by. He looked up, made eye contact with her, and she smiled at him. At that moment, he wasn't sure what had happened, but all of his sadness and bad feelings just vanished at that moment. He smiled back, and she continued on her way. They never spoke, though if they had, that would have opened up some new possibilities.

Say "Hi"

Even if somebody's just walking by, you can say, "hello, how are you?" See how they respond. You'd be surprised that nine out of ten times when you say hello to somebody, they'll smile and say "hello" back to you. And, if this is someone who you think is attractive, it opens up the possibility of a conversation that leads to you asking them out. Try this as an act of kindness with no expectations and see how people respond. It will tell you a lot about someone based on their response. I always say that the right person will respond in kind, and the wrong person will respond negatively or not at all.

Now You're Talking!

People want the kind of connection that you're bringing to them in conversation. In fact, they need those moments of contact daily. I do this all the time. I talk to people at my work, and everywhere I go. If I'm in the elevator with someone, I'll turn and ask, "so, how are you?" I don't know the person, but still, I'll ask "how are ya? Are you having a good day?" I joke around sometimes.

If they've had a rough day, I'll try to cheer them up. For the most part, people I talk to this way become more open, and it's fantastic! I like to pay compliments to people just out of the blue, especially if I see somebody who I imagine doesn't feel good about themselves. I'll say something nice to them only to perk up their feelings. It's a good feeling to do beautiful things for people.

It builds you up, too. You get to experience yourself as a good person, to declare, "I've got all this to share, so I'm going to share it!" And now, not only are you sharing kindness, but you are also opening the door for the right people to walk into your life literally anywhere you go.

Of course, as with everything else, you might occasionally get somebody who gives you a weird look or something, but that's nothing compared to the proper responses right? It just builds up your confidence, even more, to handle dealing with rejection. And those who do not respond well? Guess what they are dealing with? Their own issues (limiting beliefs), so again this has nothing to do with you.

This kind of practice helps to reprogram you, undo any of those seeds of limiting beliefs, those old bits of negative self- image where you feel small and shy. It's terrific, whether or not you get a date out of it!

The Rejection Game

If you're up for something more intense, I invite you to play the Rejection Game. This exercise was initially intended for men who are worried about making the first move because they think the rejection will be too painful.

Of course, anyone can play if they want to work on their shyness, develop their skills at approaching and meeting strangers, and reduce the fear of rejection that holds us back from so many wonderful things in life. Because my experience comes predominantly from helping men who want to master their fear of rejection, I'll talk about this in those terms.

It's straightforward: go out one night and say, "okay, I want to be rejected 40 times, and I want to see how people respond to me ." That's it. You're not going out to get numbers or even a date. You're setting out specifically to have people say "no" to you, over and over again. And yes, keep score. Set a real target and then try to achieve it before you come home for the night. Don't rush this part, it is not a race.

The Rejection Game does two things. First, it shows you how people respond to you, which says something about their worlds, their experiences, and a little bit of what it's like to walk in their shoes. You can get an understanding of how they've been conditioned. Maybe they've had some really negative experiences that stayed with them, or perhaps they have the same issues that you might have had - insecurity, lack of confidence - and they're not sure what to do with someone making the first move. The second and most important thing that the Rejection Game does is show you who's going to be more open. The wrong person for you will not respond in your favor, but the right person will. Then it just becomes a process of elimination. Expect nothing during this trial exercise, and you will most likely be happily surprised.

No matter how they respond to you, by playing the Rejection Game full out, you're going to get a first-hand understanding of how people accepting or rejecting you doesn't necessarily have anything to do with you. It's research, and trust me, research never looked more fun! You have to get dressed up and go on the town just to meet people with no attachments to what happens. You're going out to talk to people for the sake of talking to people.

This also gives you some practice at breaking the ice, which is a big challenge for many people in most social situations. Have something genuinely honest, fun, or funny to say with your approach. Here are some great examples in case you feel a little lost for words.

"Hello, you look very beautiful tonight. I have no agenda here whatsoever, but I did want to come over and let you know."

Or, "Hello, I don't really have any cheesy pick-up line. I just noticed you and wanted to come over and say hello and tell you that you're a beautiful woman. Is that okay with you?"

Gentlemen, showing some vulnerability will get you the date or at very least a kind reply from the ladies. There are many ways to choose from, but the real stuff, the honest and vulnerable thing works.

Whatever you decide to say, just be very honest, positive, friendly, and confident.

After you play the Rejection Game once or twice, you won't have any trouble approaching strangers, it could become a very normal thing for you. You're not going to take rejection personally anymore, and I guarantee you're probably going to end up with a couple of numbers. It's not going to be an issue.

Let's say you've done everything, you've recreated yourself, you go to the party, you see that special someone - or they see you. And you're feeling something good here. Now we're going to go on the first date that we've been working towards since we started this whole process.

Like attracts like. This is a fundamental law of the Universe and how people relate to each other. You want to attract desirable partners, you have to become desirable to those good-looking partners, right? But I'm not just talking about looks.

When we say that someone is "out of our league," we often use it to mean that we're trying to ask someone out who's much better looking than we are. However, it's not the looks necessarily, but that aura, that energy, that you emit in all directions. So, if you're somebody confident, in good shape, who knows what they want and will take actions to get it, you're going to start looking for others who can support or match that energy.

I find that people who were raised a certain way were taught respect and the differences between men and women. They do the right things, and people respond appropriately. A man and a woman are different entities, we need different things. This is something that needs to be acknowledged and accepted by both partners. If you allow yourself to be vulnerable, you're definitely going to connect. It's merely a trust thing.

When it comes to dating, if you try to protect yourself from the bad, you're also going to protect yourself from all the good. You're going to find reasons why you shouldn't go out with that person because you're scared. It's fear, right? Fears are going to get in the way, and you're no longer going to allow yourself to be vulnerable. You're going to be guarded, which creates negative energy. This will lead you to create excuses for why you're single or sabotage every new opportunity for love because you don't want to feel that pain. But at the end of the day, pain is part of life.

You're going to feel pain anyway, but you can at least choose to control the amount of pain that you're going to have. And when it comes to love, short-term pain can sometimes lead to a long-term payoff in finding a love that lasts.

Dating Online

Now let's touch on online dating.

We're busy professionals. We're tired at night from all of the strenuous activities we've been doing by day. We want to meet somebody, but we just don't have the time or space in our heads to make that happen. On the other hand, we don't want to be alone, and we do want to be able to have the opportunity to meet somebody. That's why online dating is so popular, though not without its own share of problems.

In this day and age, almost everyone's got an agenda. It's quite a task to try to decipher what's real and what's not. But there's an efficient way to go through your available options, no matter which online dating site you decide to use.

First, don't consider pictures where people are wearing sunglasses, are shirtless or are trying to model their bodies without anything in their bios. Right away, you can tell it won't be a match. Those people are basing their connections on physicality, and by wearing sunglasses, they're trying to create a sense of "mystery" so you'll message them. But really, it's far more likely that they feel like they have something to hide. I also don't like pictures where the users have their friends' faces visible. Though it's good to show that you're sociable, but they should be taking the time to blur their friends' faces in any pictures they use. Online dating should just be about you and your prospective dates, not your friends.

Of course, you should use your discretion. If you see a profile where the person has a great beach body or sunglasses, and you have a good gut feeling about it, send them a message. It couldn't hurt, but just don't expect too much from the conversation.

Next, I think you should definitely look at the profiles and try to read between the lines and get a feel for who the person is and what their likes are. You can usually tell who a person is in the words that they use and how they use them. This takes a lot of time, though, because you can get lots of messages, and it can be hard to find time to message the ones that you like. However, if you see someone who's attractive who also seems to be an exciting person, reading their profile is time well-spent (plus, a lot of them are funny). If you feel someone is forthcoming or shows some vulnerability, it's usually a good sign. If they did not spend time on their profile or did not offer anything interesting about themselves to inspire you, then they are not serious about landing the right partner. Serious people do the work!

Let's say you've sent out a few messages, and now you get a reply. That's awesome! When you're online, and you've actually connected with somebody that you think you might like, don't waste your time. Get on a phone call within a couple of days. The people who don't take dating seriously tend to keep all of their interactions on the online dating site, while the people who are serious and who are the best matches for you know that the dating site is just a starting point. If they need a little more time to be comfortable with a phone call, that's fine, but make sure that you get a chance to stop emailing and start talking quickly. Special note for men: if you're a man contacting a woman, they'll want to feel safe with you before giving out their numbers.

There are a lot of creepers out there, and you'll have to show that you're not one of them. Just be patient and do what you can to show your genuine compassion to the women you message.

Phone calls force you to chat in real time, which means the answers that you give to questions and the things that you say can show more about who you really are. You won't have time to perfect what you say the way that you can with emails. Plus, with a phone call, you get to hear the person's tone. Which, as Will Smith's character in Hitch points out, carries 20% of your communication. You'll simply have a stronger impression from talking than emailing or texting.

How do you set up a phone call with your online dating prospect? First, send a text to the other person to connect the number and introduce yourself via text. This is important because now you've moved off the dating site itself. That's something that many daters who aren't serious and play games with people don't do, so you've shown yourself as someone who's committed to finding something real.

Next, set up a time for a call so that you have no distractions so you can really focus on the individual and get to know them. Setting up calls for when one or both of you is driving is not only unsafe (keep your eyes on the road!) but also says that you're not considerate enough to give the other person your full attention.

During the call, be present to the details, big and small. Do you get a sense that they're really listening to you? That they're truthful? How does it feel to talk to them? Do they seem genuine? Most of all, are you both having fun?

If the phone call goes well, ask for their last name and then offer to have another phone call later in the week. While you're waiting, make sure that they are who they say they are. Google them, go to LinkedIn, check to see if they have a profile. If they check out, and if that second phone call goes really well, make sure you set up a coffee date before you hang up.

If, after your call, you'll realize if you actually want to meet them or you don't. Make your decisions quickly and go with your gut feeling. Anybody that puts you off or continues to e-mail you and continues the conversation online, there's something not right about that.

Rules of Engagement

So, let's say you've met someone casually, whether online or in person. You've sensed that vibe, you're feeling terrific about it, and you decide to have a first date. What do you do?

Remember a few things as you go into the dating experience. Be Presentable. First things first, remember your self-image.

By this time, you've already got a dazzling wardrobe of beautiful clothes that brings out the best in you, whether it's a casual stroll in jeans or a sharp-looking jacket or cocktail dress for a formal party. For your date, dressing up is a non-issue: you're going to look great! Of course, you don't have to dress up to the nines this time. Depending on whether it's dinner at a fancy restaurant or a show of some kind, make sure to be presentable. Look good, smell good. Ladies, wear your heels. Men, look sharp, make sure the ladies can notice your cologne, and walk with confidence (head up, shoulders back). If your hair is scraggly, get a quick haircut beforehand. In the past, this was seen as "trying too hard," but in the current era where most people are super-casual (and usually just playing around), nobody works hard on how they look. Getting groomed before your first date shows that you consider the date important. Not only that, you will feel good and boost your energy, helping you send out more of that vibe.

Remember your chivalry. Open the doors, pull out chairs, even stand up when the lady approaches the table, which will blow her mind.

Listen more than speak. This especially applies to men. Get to know your date, hear what they're saying and think about it, then respond. Don't try to change the subject back to yourself every third or fourth sentence, engage with what the other person wants to talk about until they ask about you.

Have fun! No matter what, this is about letting life lead you where you need to be led. This is what you need to have to move forward in the right direction. Have no expectations, no assumptions, and no reactions. Time will tell you everything about the person.

Don't be needy. Being needy comes from limiting beliefs. It's how you were raised or can originate in past disappointments. They're not attractive. Everyone wants a confident person to some degree, and those who are needy are people who have been deprived emotionally and are a little hungry. They're starved for love. A little bit of attention will gradually fill up their cup and ease some of that anxiety. But more to the point, it says that the other person may need to do the kind of inner work that you've been doing to fill themselves up with positivity and satisfaction, so they don't need to get it primarily through a relationship.

They may need to become the Total Package themselves. And if you find yourself feeling needy at that moment, don't worry: that's just your limiting beliefs popping up!

For your first in-person date, you'll want to have a good part of it where you can continue your conversations, but also some components where you can get up and do something. For this reason, a coffee date followed by a nice walk downtown, or something like mini-putt or some other activity works. If you're really feeling like physical exercise, rock-climbing and bike ride on nature trails have become popular options over the years. Or, if you're more relaxed, there's no beating the classic dinner and a movie, plus a quick dessert or coffee stop afterward to talk about how well you liked the show.

Whatever the first date is like, stay present. This is the first time you and your prospective partner are interacting in the flesh. This is where you'll see the early signs of physical attraction.

You'll have things in common right from the start, and you'll also be pretty different. Let the conversation flow, but remember to ask the critical questions for this "getting to know you" stage. Are your parents still together? What was your childhood like? Where did you grow up? What do you like doing? Have fun with it!

One caveat: don't ask any heavy questions about past relationships. Unless they bring it up (and if they do bring it up frequently, it could be a sign they still need some time to process and let go), stay focused on the present. If your date goes well, set up your second one when you get home, one that maybe appeals to an interest that your date mentioned while you were out together. If you're in flow - if the conversations are easy and fun, if you find each other fascinating - every subsequent date will simply add to the magic and the energy between the two of you.

If your date doesn't go well, or if some of that early magic wears off way too fast, that's okay. Neither of you owes anything to each other, other than respect and sincerity. Be polite and honest, call the other person, and tell them the truth: it isn't working out, and though you're glad to have met them, it's probably best that you continue searching for the right person. If you feel that they're a really cool person with whom you want to stay friends, definitely ask them if friendship appeals to them as well. If it does, you've gained a friend! And if not, wish them well... .then start messaging other people on your dating site.

Eventually, maybe after one or two tries, perhaps after a few, you'll find someone who'll spark something that lasts, and you can close down your dating profile for good.

In my matchmaking business, we match people in three different categories, and I would strongly suggest you incorporate this process into your profiling when meeting new people.

The first category is your character, which is built on your values and previous experiences in life (for example, how you were raised, painful or joyful experiences you've been through, etc. .).

The second one is your personality. If you're outgoing and adventurous and an extrovert, you are best suited with the same type of character, someone who shares those personality traits and commonalities.

The third category is your lifestyle. For example, if you have grown children and you meet someone who has very young children, you might be in different places in your life, and it might not be a fit. Maybe you travel a lot for work, and the other person is ready to retire. Or, perhaps you want to travel, and you meet someone who has a career, who is a 9 to 5 or is starting up a company. If you're someone who's very spiritual and continually takes programs or is into personal growth and development, you would definitely want to meet a like-minded person, someone who shares that lifestyle and mindset.

Not everything has to be the same, of course. It's good to have some differences as well, but the core values of the person should line up with yours.

Basically, these are the ways that the whole world conditions you to become the person who you are. The same applies to your prospective partners.

Take note of some of the "deal-breaker" things as you continue your courtship. If you're somebody who wants to have a family, obviously you need to meet somebody of age who wants the same things that you do. You have to be on the same page. That's how lifestyle works. If you meet somebody and you fall in love, and they're a little bit older, they might already have kids, or they might not want to have kids, but you do. If you don't want to miss out on that aspect of your life, then it's probably not going to work.

One perspective I provide to some potential male clients looking to find a younger woman to date is that in ten years, she can trade them in for a newer model and potentially take half of what they built. What are they left with at that point?

Because now, they're not 60, they're 70, and their options have gotten a lot smaller.

You have to decide what your priority is: that relationship or having a child. Base your decision on that, as those things have to line up, too. You can't be a 9-5er dating an entrepreneur who wants to travel the world unless they're prepared to take you under their wing and provide the security that allows you to feel safe quitting your job. If they love you, they might want to provide that opportunity for you to be able to leave your work and focus on the relationship.

Professional Matchmaking

Is meeting people in person too much of a hassle? Not really feeling online dating? Another option that might be up your alley is matchmaking.

Matchmaking was the old school way of dating, way back in the day. People would just put other people together. It's one of the oldest professions and it still very much exists in different cultures - Arab, Jewish, Persian, and Indian cultures in particular - with many of the relatives doing the actual matchmaking. Still, these people aren't necessarily intuited with how things would work between two particular people. There are arranged marriages, there are mail-order brides, there are all kinds of things.

Now because of how much things have changed in the last couple of decades - there's more technology, more disconnect, less interpersonal development, less communication like the eyes and the minds connecting - how are single people ever going to connect? In many cases, they can't, so they have to make those right choices for themselves. What kind of partner do you want to have? What type of foundation do you want to have?

If you know what you want and how you want it, you go to a matchmaker. Matchmakers have a pool of people who feel the same way and are looking for similar connections. I can line up ten, twenty, or however, many people in front of you that you already know are going to be able to relate to you. They've had the same experiences, or they've also done the work, or they also take care of their body the same way that you do. Each person has enough similarities to you that you can understand each other. You'll also have that physical attraction from the start because the matchmaker will have pictures, and your first contact will often be the first date that your matchmaker will set up for you.

Hiring a matchmaker eliminates the trial-and-error of dating. You're going to get to that relationship a lot quicker. Of course, whether or not you connect is up to you. But just as with regular dating or online dating, if it doesn't work out, there's someone else waiting in the wings.

What qualities should you look for in a matchmaker? You have to find somebody who can relate to you, who can also understand, who's got a great perception and be able to identify those people. It's good to interview a few different matchmakers and also create a relationship and work with somebody who you trust, who you feel has the ability and the confidence to go after the right people and who is personable, because you have to constantly find people that are on the same wavelength.

Not all matchmakers are the same. I would suggest finding somebody who's intuitive, who's very personable, and who really cares about making a difference because that's going to be key.

(If you want to find out how we do it, please visit www.perfect-fit.ca - Everything is there for you).

15 Things to Keep in Mind for The First Date

First dates are always exciting, but the expectation of meeting Mr. or Ms. Right can also be a little unnerving. Women tend to overthink every detail about the date, from what to wear to what they will eat. However, a good date should be easy and fun, and come with no expectations. With that said, sometimes it is hard to tell what your date is thinking, if a person is being genuine, or if they have another agenda. So here are fifteen things to keep in mind on the first date.

1. Asking Permission.

A man should never assume you will go out with him. He should ask for your permission. It shows he respects you and that he is willing to be turned down if you say no. He allows the decision to be yours, and that's confidence! If someone asks you out over a text, you may need to tell him to go back to the "Rules of Engagement" drawing board.

Ladies, men like yes or no answers, so try not to make them chase you if you like him.

2. All we have is our word.

Integrity, especially integrity with one's word, is everything. As author Don Miguel Ruiz writes in The Four Agreements, "be impeccable with your word". Communication isn't just saying, it's doing what you say you're going to do. Keep your word when you make promises to meet somewhere or call someone. These little things are essential and will establish your character for the potential relationship. Trust me, they are paying attention to these small things.

How well does your date follow through on what they say? The red flag here is if they routinely promise to do something, then fail to keep that promise. It starts with calling, not just texting: you want to hear their tone as well as their words. When setting up a date, do they sound direct and to the point, or are they elusive and tight-lipped? Do they seem happy to be speaking to you, or always annoyed or in a hurry ("I can't talk long!"). These are clues as to what you can expect to happen next. Take this time to ask the key questions of your potential partner (in a funny, light-hearted way, of course).

3. Dressing Well and Attention to Detail.

When it comes to getting a date, first impressions are everything. I call them "the hook," but it's what the person does after getting your attention that counts. Personalities will always set the stage for the type of date you will have.

A well-dressed date who smells good is always a turn on. When a woman can see that a man has put some effort into his preparation for a date and vice versa, it makes a great first impression. A date that looks like they don't care about themselves will probably also care less about you.

You might be initially interested in how they look, but what about their substance? If they're immature or shallow, that might be a deal-breaker right from the start. How do they treat you? What kind of character do they demonstrate? These are vital questions, so while you're on the date, you should pay special attention to the little details. Do they hold out the chair for you? Offer you a drink? Pay you compliments or hold open the door? How do they treat the wait-staff at the restaurant or the barista at the coffee shop? No matter how attractive they may look, these are the details to watch for.

4.   Active Listening.

Try not to talk too much without allowing the other person the opportunity to share about themselves. Listen and ask fun personality questions instead of heavy ones. The first date is all about fun and lightness.

One of the biggest complaints in many relationships is that the other person just doesn't listen! That's not true of everyone, of course, and in many cases, your partner's attentiveness is a good indicator of their commitment to the relationship. The first two or three dates are the best times to test this out. Are they listening to what you're saying to them? Do they ask about you? Those are two excellent signs. If you have kids from a previous relationship, do they ask about them, and their other parent? That's a perfect sign that your date may be a good match because those questions show that they're looking to see how they fit into your life. Pay attention to how much attention they pay you in the places that count.

5. Kind Gestures.

Kind gestures don't have to be big, dramatic actions, but little things. The way that your partner does something special for you without any expectation in return. It could be buying you a small item that you mentioned off-hand you wanted to have, or taking you to a restaurant for a dish that you enjoy. It shows that they're listening to you and paying attention.

Here's one example I often see in my business. What happened to the men that would call or come and knock on your door? Instead, we get men that text you when he is in your driveway. These days, if you find a man that comes to your door, or brings you flowers, then he is a winner and chances are he was taught correctly by his parents. It should be a given that he holds open the door for you. If he doesn't, then keep your eyes open, as he may not be a good fit. There needs to be something about your date that captures you.

6. Location.

The best place for a first date is somewhere low key and intimate. Going for coffee, at a local coffee shop, is an excellent way for both parties to get to know each other and be comfortable. A dinner or activity date is also a great first date idea. The key is to make it light and fun. The location or experience really depends on the man and how they would like to entertain their lady. It's a personal preference, one that's really up to the couple. Overall, an easy-going attitude is best.

7. Conversation.

The conversation is very important, and it should not be serious. You want curiosity questions about your life or your day. Just note: DO NOT INTERVIEW! That goes for you and your date. Interviews make people nervous, and a suitable date should not make you uncomfortable or nervous in any way. Just be yourself, have fun, and have no expectations. This mindset keeps the disappointment out of your way during your process. Dating is a numbers game if you want to be efficient in meeting The One. Having no expectations will always make things lighter and leave room for pleasant surprises.

What do you talk about, then? Asking about your prospective partner's career helps you get a sense of their world and personality. An artist has a different set of skills and interests compared to someone who sells insurance.

Don't worry about how much they make: your focus is on how their career influences them as a person, which may or may not be compatible with you and your life.

8.   No Drama.

You do not want to hear about someone's drama on the first date. The baggage should be left behind. You want to get to know the person and not all their problems. If a person continues to talk about their past, they will always live in the past, and it will be a turn off for someone new. Also, it's essential to be a good listener and show interest in what your date is sharing.

9.   Joking Around.

A good sense of humor is super attractive! Anyone that can poke fun at themselves is a keeper. You want to laugh and joke around with each other during and after the date. It gives you both a chance to unwind, bring your guard down and be yourselves.

10.   Eye Contact.

Maintaining eye contact shows interest in the other person. A date that keeps eye contact shows that they are confident and it creates a connection. Also, the eye is naturally drawn to something (or someone, hint hint) it finds pleasing.

11. Not Glued to Phone.

Your date should only be paying attention to you. If you find your candidate checking their phone or texting in the middle of your date, not only is that rude, but it also shows they do not respect you enough. If they have children, it's okay to have the phone close by, but the attention should be on the date. If it's necessary to be connected during your date, at the very least put it on vibrate and maybe check it when you go to the restroom.

12. Overall Impression.

Trust your gut! If you are having a great time and have good feelings about your date, share this with them. If you feel uncomfortable in any way, still be respectful until the end of the date, and continue the journey as it is a process of elimination. Know what you want, what you are looking for, and go after it. Find a person that rocks your socks off and have lots of fun dating while you are at it!

13. Making the Second Date.

If you both enjoyed the date, make the second date right away. No point in playing any games if you both are on the same page.

14. The Third Date.

It usually takes about three dates to get a good feeling for a potential candidate. Some people know right away, but the three-date rule will keep you diligent in making the right decision on the match.

15. Intimacy.

If you have incredible chemistry with a date that makes you feel like ripping your clothes off, be careful with this. If you both go for it, you create the risk of things blowing up. Several components may bite you in the ass if you move too fast. Let's say you both jump into bed. There is a form of commitment that comes with jumping into bed right away if both people are serious about finding someone long term. If you decide to get intimate quickly make sure both of you discuss the moment and there is a follow through. Lots of people jump the gun without thinking and then backpedal.

Chapter 7

MAINTAINING YOUR RELATIONSHIP

"Life is 10 % what happens to you and 90% how you react to it."

How does it feel to have it all?

If all has gone well, you've woken up this morning beside the partner of your dreams. Only it's not a dream, it's your reality. This is what Total Package Living looks like!

At this point, there's not much else to do but continue to follow your powerful routines. Stay fit, keep your space and friendships uncluttered and empowering, and maintain what you've created.

Of course, you've got to maintain your relationship as well. This chapter is all about making sure that you don't lose that spark.

Basic Practices

Here are some of the most important things that you should keep at the top of your list while being in the relationship:

- Listen more than you speak. Your turn to speak will come. When someone else is speaking, listen without interrupting.
- Practice empathy. Try to put yourself in their shoes when you're having conversations, so you can really understand how that person feels.
- Have a date night at least once a week.
- Show your love and appreciation all the time, even if you don't feel like it.
- Try not to smother the other person. Remember, you're supposed to have a life of your own within the relationship. Remember not to lose yourself in the

relationship, and don't give them a reason to lose themselves in the relationship.

- Keep your other friendships and family time going while you're in the relationship.
- Remember that you may share a common foundation, but each person ought to have their own interests and hobbies. If you like to cook and they like to make things out of clay, you cook, and let them make things out of clay. Just because you met doesn't mean that you should stop doing what you love. Everyone's entitled to be their own person within the relationship.
- Never go to bed angry.
- Never point the finger. Deliver your communications in a way that's gentle and easily-received, wherever possible.

The Hard Truth of Commitment

All of these practices and more create a relationship that's rich, loving, and respectful. That being said, none of these practices, either together or on their own, can guarantee that you'll be together forever. This is a straightforward reality of all relationships that almost no one talks about: people can abandon ship at any time.

In the film (500) Days of Summer, Tom (Joseph Gordon-Levitt) says, in a moment of fear, to his love interest/friend Summer (Zooey Deschanel), "I need to know that you're not going wake up in the morning and feel differently." Summer, who's unsure about him, replies "And I can't give you that. Nobody can."

Every day is a choice to be with that person, whether or not you make it consciously. Anyone can abandon ship at any time. This is a harsh reality to accept, especially if you're used to typical Hollywood romances, but it is the truth.

Friendships with Other People

As a woman, can you be friends with a man who is not your boyfriend if you're in a relationship? And vice versa? Sure, but they need to be friends with your partner. (I'm using cisgender and heterosexual language here, but this also applies to same-sex, non-binary couples).

If they don't want to be friends with your partner, maybe they like you more than you think. Could be a wolf in sheep's clothing, or perhaps they just really like you. It's very possible to meet other people outside of your relationship that you also have that energy with, which takes you back to your commitments. You've made a commitment to this person, and you need to stick to it. The grass is not necessarily greener on the other side. If you leave something good for what you think is something better, remember that there are a lot of limiting beliefs behind the scenes that you won't see at first.

And what if you are curious? If you see something in your friend that you're not getting from your partner, that may say something about your needs. Before you do anything outwards, go inward and ask, "what is it about me that's attracted to this quality in this person that I think I'm not getting from my partner?" And then, have that conversation with your partner, which takes us back to honesty. I'd rather hear the truth and deal with a little bit of pain and conflict than stick my head in the sand and be blindsided entirely down the line. I'd rather hear the truth and have the opportunity to fix it.

And if you're worried that such a conversation might end your relationship, remember that staying in a relationship is a choice you make every day.

Friendships with other people with whom you share that kind of energy are possible, provided you don't cross that boundary. If you know that this is bothering your partner, your loyalty is to your partner. It's not a bad thing that they feel that way because they are human. It's okay to feel insecure or threatened from time to time. That doesn't mean that there's anything wrong there. Your commitment, the right choice, would be to take care of your partner to whom you've committed.

If the reason why you're reading this book is because you got cheated on, this is obviously bringing up some powerful limiting beliefs for you and your traumas. Understanding this dynamic is important because, just as no one is perfect, it's very unlikely that you're going to have a relationship where these feelings of betrayal don't come up again. Your partner is also as free as you are to walk anytime, and that's an uncomfortable concept to get. But if you understand, have trust and communication, and you still find yourself with a partner who does something similar, you'll be okay to have those conversations. Him or her having a friend will not necessarily end in disaster if you remember and affirm your original commitments to each other, if you respect your partner, and you put them first because you love them.

If you find that the wounds that you had from infidelity or past relationships aren't healing easily, don't hesitate to speak to a professional therapist, relationship counselor, or coach.

And, if you have that conversation with your partner and they don't take it well, you can agree to disagree, and maybe part ways amicably and with love. It never has to be a disaster. If someone wants to leave you, but they've been honest with you, you might be heartbroken, but you'll respect their decision. Honesty is their way of respecting you. And if you were to end this relationship that wasn't fulfilling you, you're reconnecting with the life that you created before you met them.

Remember, too, that maybe all of this happened for a reason or a season, out of your direct control. Perhaps the Universe created this relationship as a shorter experience, to put you in a position for something greater down the line.

How Technology is Destroying the Fabric of Relationships

As much as we love technology - it's impressive, convenient, great for work and keeping us connected on some level with each other - when it comes to humanity, it's destroying the human aspect of interaction. We are trading the rich experience of life and relationships with each other for the convenience of electronic connection. Our skills and interactions with other people are removed from real context. All we have left is a technological device where, if you're texting, you don't see their expressions or hear their voice, and you eliminate that from your life. How, then, are you going to cultivate that ability to read people? To make your own impression on them? To build relationships with them...using a device? How will you spot the wolf in sheep's clothing?

Communication experts have said that 70 to 75% of human communication is body language, and anywhere between 15-20% is your tone. That means that only 5 to 10% of communication is your words, but the technology of texting and emails is only words. People have known this for a long time, but they communicate this way anyway, knowing what they're missing. Why? Simple, it's an addiction.

Tech companies have created this addiction by design. We are now bringing our beliefs and experiences to these devices and allowing them to program us. We see images and ideas on computers and phones and forget about the beauty of flesh and blood people. The tech companies want you to engage as much with their platforms and devices as possible. They're all making money, and they don't want you to leave.

What does that do to your relationships? Your trust? Faith? Commitments? You may have a partner who's terrific for you, but you may then see a profile of someone where they're only showing you their best qualities, and you might think that the grass is greener. With so many options, we are being taught to give up on relationships instead of value them and fight for them. You may end something good and real to chase a mirage. Technology is also creating a breeding ground for misconceptions, assumptions, and wrong expectations. Now, when you get a text message, you don't hear the tone or see the expression, but you make an assumption of how they are sending the message, often fueled by your limiting beliefs.

The solution? Stop using it. Or, at least, stop using technology when it matters that you are with another human being.

Don't talk about anything important or heavy over the phone or by email. Have the talk in person where you can get 100% of the person's communication. Technology can be misinterpreted by your significant other. You get an innocuous message from a friend, and because they saw a Facebook post earlier that day that talked about how some other cheater was caught, they now have it in their minds that you might be cheating. You want technology to work for you, you don't want to work for the technology. That's a decision that you can make. Because so much of this technology is new, the solution actually lies in what we now consider old beliefs, which I loosely call chivalry.

(And we don't even want to talk about what technology does to your sleep, attention span, radiation, eyesight, and other health issues that you might not realize are caused by your devices.)

Kids and Relationships

When you both have kids, the relationship needs to come first. Somewhere down the line, if all goes well, and if the Universe intends for it, you'll find yourself having children with your partner. At that point, your life will change forever. I say that as a mother.

Pregnancy and childbirth will definitely throw off your routine, no matter what. That's fine, you've got to focus on Mommy and baby's needs. Once you have kids, however, you need to put your old routine back into motion.

After six months, you find yourself juggling child-rearing, changing diapers, feedings, helping them to sleep, and so on. It's very easy to forget your old patterns and commitments to each other. Reinstate Date Night as quickly as possible. You'll be pulled in different directions all the time anyway, so don't wait until the perfect time to get back to your old habits. And this is very much a part of child-raising: your children need to grow up and see their parents in love. This is where those beliefs about the world and relationships will be planted. They need to experience healthy relationships within their own lives as they are growing up. You'll be the guide to creating and modeling that healthy pattern for them for when they grow up.

Conclusion

Well, we've come to the end of our journey together, and as with any journey, it's good to take a moment to pause and look back at how far you've come, and then maybe talk a bit about what's ahead.

If you followed this program as instructed, you've spent a very vigorous six months from when you started to right now. Take a look back at who you were, what your life was like, what your physical health was like, and what your friendships and relationships were like when you started this book.

How much of a difference do you see? Do you recognize yourself on the other side of this process? Most importantly, are you happy with who you see in the mirror?

As I said in the beginning, becoming the Total Package wasn't going to be an overnight transformation, it was going to be baby steps, steps which you've now taken. And if you've skipped ahead, as some people tend to do, then I'd suggest you go back and follow this book with integrity. The truth of the matter is, you think you don't have time, but you do, and there is no better use of your time than to live in integrity.

As motivational speaker Jay Shetty says so eloquently, we don't waste money the way that we waste time. If 86,400 seconds were dollar bills that you were given every day that was going to get used up no matter what by the time the clock struck midnight, you would never waste those dollars the way that you waste your time. The truth is, there's never going to be a "good time" to get started with this transformation.

Procrastination is something that happens when you have one or more limiting beliefs that are keeping you from action. You know what there is to do, you know why you want to do it, but the trick is that knowing what you need to do doesn't mean you'll do it. As with any outcome, the key to doing the thing is doing the thing!

If you've reached the end of this program and you have done what I've taught you, then you should congratulate and acknowledge yourself for having done what 95% of the population never does, and actually take action. You have transformed your life. You've given yourself your own power in this place called life. You've become the Total Package.

And remember why I called it the "total package ." This isn't simply to find love in the form of a relationship. It wasn't only to become the perfect partner for your ideal partner: it was also about the love of self, love of integrity, and most of all, the love of living to your fullest.

Look at your life now. Every day, you eat healthy food and exercise your body. You wake up and perform your own ritual - a prayer, an invocation, a meditation, what have you - that reaffirms that vision of the greatest version of yourself so far. You live in an inviting space that is full of positive energy, that charges you up and gets you excited for what's to come in any given day. Your relationships are thriving. You know how to keep those who empower, enlighten, and love you the most, closest to you. And you've learned to keep those who are good for some things, but not necessarily the most positive, at a fair distance, in a way that ensures that you both show up as your best selves for each other.

You've taken responsibility for how you present yourself to the world, not necessarily by wearing the flashiest clothes or sporting the shiniest shoes but wearing clothes that reflect your best self-image, in a way that makes others take notice of who you are.

You've also come to understand that every person walking the planet is in their own little box world where they perceive things differently based on their own past experiences. This will help you understand why some people will take the steps that you have while others won't, why some people energize you and lift you up while others don't, and most of all, why some people become your soul-mates and others go away.

If you were already in a relationship when you started becoming the Total Package, the odds are pretty good that you've transformed your relationship to something more vivacious, juicy, passionate, and empowering for the both of you. Or maybe you've parted ways with those partners who you needed to leave, who weren't able or willing, for their own reasons, to stay with you and create something and that's fine too.

Maybe, in the course of doing this work, you have found the man or woman of your dreams. (Maybe you didn't wake up alone today?)

If you've done the work and are still searching for the one, remember, they will see your light shining at the other end of the room, and know that it's you that they've been looking for all of their lives. Keep putting yourself out there in person. Keep sending those messages. Stay in your integrity and keep at it. When the timing of the Universe is right, you will meet your Mister or Miss Right.

(Of course, if you want to speed up that process, you'll find resources and details on matchmaking services that my company, Perfect Fit, can provide you, should you want them!)

I want to thank you for letting me lead you on this journey, and I want to suggest one last thing: pay it forward.

Where does all of this go from here? You have your whole life ahead of you now as the best version of yourself, and I can tell you that there is always a greater version just waiting to emerge. They say you can't get there from here. Meaning, you can't get to Point C from Point A: you have to reach Point B first. Now that you've reached this new level of growth, there's an even greater version of you that lies ahead that's now within your reach. If you think that you're now fulfilled, I will invite you to expand your life even further. The way that you do that is to contribute that energy, positivity, and love beyond yourself and your life to others.

What makes some of the most attractive people on the planet that much more appealing is that they know what they're here to do. This is something that not a lot of people have. And you don't need this, but I would suggest that if you haven't found out what you're here to do, you should start looking into it. A great motivational speaker, Les Brown, put it best, "the problem with people isn't that they aim high and miss, it's that they aim low and hit ."

By completing this process, you've already demonstrated that you can aim high and hit, and there's still more that you can do. Get involved in your community, reach out to those friends who are in need. Give some of this abundance that you feel to someone else today. It doesn't have to be money or time.

Smile at people. Brighten someone's day, the way you learned in this program. Pay it all forward.

The fact is, we live in a time of chaos and negativity everywhere we look, and you don't want to add to that. You don't want to be in a negative space, so why not take what you've created and work to transform the world around you, showing up in the realities of other people as someone who creates possibilities, a teacher for others to learn from.

Maybe you have a far more ambitious goal in mind that you can now reach in this new version of yourself that you couldn't reach when you started this program. Whether it's starting a company, setting up a non-profit to help at-risk youth or rescue animals; whether it's saving the environment or running for office, or even something as modest as volunteering your time in a soup kitchen, or making sure that your elderly neighbors are okay. Whatever it happens to be for you, if you've set a lofty goal for yourself, I'd suggest that now is the time for you to go for it.

As Jay Shetty says:

To realize the value of one year, ask a student who failed a grade.

To realize the value of one month, ask a mother who lost their child in the final month.

To realize the value of one week, ask the editor of an online magazine.

To realize the value of one hour, ask the couple who's in a long-distance relationship.

To realize the value of one minute, ask the person who just missed a bus, train, or plane.

To realize the value of one second, ask the person who just missed an accident.

And to realize the value of a millisecond, ask the person who just came second at the Olympics.

Life and time are the best two teachers. Life teaches us to make good use of time, and time teaches us the value of life.

Where do you go from here? The sky really is the limit, and your time to push that limit is now!

Aviva (January 2019)

Testimonials

Life Changing

"Aviva guided me through my marriage separation and helped me cope with my feelings, overcome my situation, and move onto the next stage in my life. If you or anyone you know is looking for life coaching, matchmaking, or fitness advice, Aviva can do it all in a very professional and personal way. She is truly involved with your life and cares about you and your results. She will direct you to the tools you need to make positive changes in your life." – Don

Great Coach!

Need to look no further than Aviva! She is dedicated to you and you get a full-on approach on how to love yourself and attract the right person. Aviva is dedicated to finding the right person for you! She is an amazing life coach who gets you into the right frame of mind and sets you on the right path! - AM

Aviva helps make meaningful life-changing connections!

Aviva pointed me to my future the night she introduced me to my queen and love, Racquel, at one of her mixer events. I found out later that Aviva had already made the calculation that Racquel and I would hit it off if we connected, and she was right! She saw it even before we did and we couldn't be more grateful to her and her instincts for helping people make meaningful life-changing connections. Now we are building a life and family together filled with all the blessings that can only come from bringing the two right people together. - Jason

A great coach!
I met Aviva from Perfect Fit in the fall of 2014. I had a few interviews with her and immediately became a client. That's how comfortable she made me feel. I went to a couple of her events - which were so very fun! - and she had so many nice people attending them. Shortly after, Aviva introduced me to the beautiful classy woman who I am currently in a relationship with, and we are very happy together! She is exactly the type of woman I've been looking for! I recommend Aviva and Perfect Fit to anyone looking for love and a committed relationship. It's worth it! - Nick

Best High-End Dating Service in the GTA!
If you are a high end (or wealthy) executive and looking for a high-end dating service in the GTA, look no further. Aviva's experience, knowledge, connections, and passion to help bring love into the busy lives of successful businessmen is a definite reason for her high success rate. If you are tired of the regular avenues for meeting women, you should definitely consider Perfect Fit and invest in yourself. - Joel

Transformed

I hired Perfect Fit firm for personal training. It took about a year's time to get into the shape that I needed to be, and I'm finally in the best shape in my life. Aviva is great to work with: very knowledgeable, results-driven, and definitely knows her stuff. It was never boring: I was always looking forward to my training sessions. I would definitely recommend working with her and her company for any lifestyle services. It was a great experience! - VM

My Personal Resources & Referrals For All Your Lifestyle Needs

Jason O'Brien

In my work I aim to strike a balance of emotion and elegant humanity. I want it to be both a contemplative and poetic experience for the viewer that stirs the spirit and moves the soul.

www.jasonobriengallery.com | **@jason_obrien_gallery_live**

Email promo code **VIVA** to info@jasonobriengallery.com for a 10% discount on any limited edition print.

The Vessel Acrylic on canvas, 36 x 48 inches

GALA

FASHION FOR PASSION

Modern meets chic, where personality isn't the first thing you see.

An exclusive boutique in Toronto GALA FASHION will create, manufacture by hand, and deliver our modern jewelry and accessories all over the world. The unique cut and attractive combinations of leather, textiles and hardware are the hallmarks of our brand and give any woman a modern advantage.

Quote : "You are a good artist when you make someone's experience feel something deep or unexpected."

Anyone can create art, but not everyone can make you feel something by looking at their art. The idea of harmony underlies the philosophy of our brand - the desire for simplicity, elegance and empowerment of self-expression.

GALA MIREY

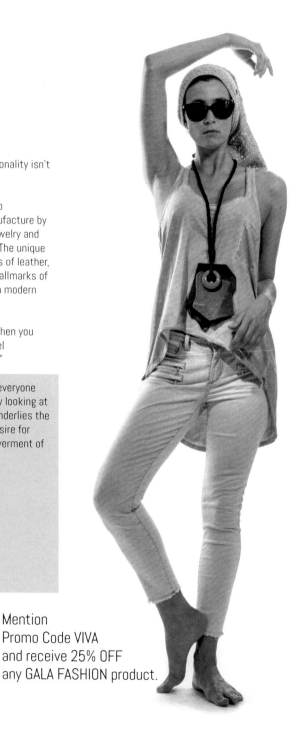

Mention
Promo Code VIVA
and receive 25% OFF
any GALA FASHION product.

galafashion.ca

N A I L S

Toronto is an ethnically diverse city with the core of soaring skyscrapers all overshadowed by the iconic CN Tower. It is a prominent place with plenty of options in entertainment, food, wellness, and particularly beauty. Within this beauty domain, is an abundance of nail shops that have transformed an industry into an entrepreneurial revolution, especially within the Vietnamese community. With so many out there, the nail business is in constant motion with how nails are being done and particularly in who does them.

Johnny Chiem, the founder of Hard Rock Nails, is a force to be reckoned with. His ability to step outside the box with his skillful technique, polish artistry, attentive care, and relaxed atmosphere has made him one of Toronto's sought out nail professional. With over 35k followers on his Instagram that showcase the work of Hard Rock Nails, his creativity along with his team shines through.

Johnny is humble as he highlights that his success is not based on him alone, but the hard work, commitment to the profession, and dedication to refining the craft because of his staffs. It is apparent the family culture he instills with everyone and that if you want to go fast, go alone but if you're going to go far, go together.

790 Broadview Avenue, Toronto, ON M4K 2P7
(Across from Broadview subway station)
416.818.8971 | hello@hardrocknails.com

Mention promo code **"VIVA"**
and receive 10% Off
your service.

DON'T JUDGE A BOOK BY IT'S COVER!

We know..... yet we all do it anyway. First impressions are extremely important. For better or for worse your audience will formulate an opinion often before you say a word.

Let Soren Custom show you how the nuances of style, colour psychology and image can contribute to an outward expression of who you truly are on the inside. Soren Custom sells suits but more importantly we sell an experience. Our made-to-measure suit experience and process is one-of-a-kind.

They say we have the best suiting experience in Toronto....we tend to agree. This is the essence of cool. We did not invent the suit, but we are passionate in our goal to pave a new path for how you connect with yours.

Its You 2.0

Book your consultation with one of our experienced stylists.

Remember, it's not a suit... It's an experience.

Esthetic Laser Clinic Inc

since 1997

High Speed Permanent
LASER HAIR REMOVAL
with customized comfort

Back and Legs can now be treated
in only 15-20 minutes!!!

Contact us at 416.930.2248 or
email at estheticlaserinc@gmail.com
www.estheticlaserclinic.ca

Mention promo code **"VIVA"**
and receive a complimentary
Laser Hair Removal Treatment.

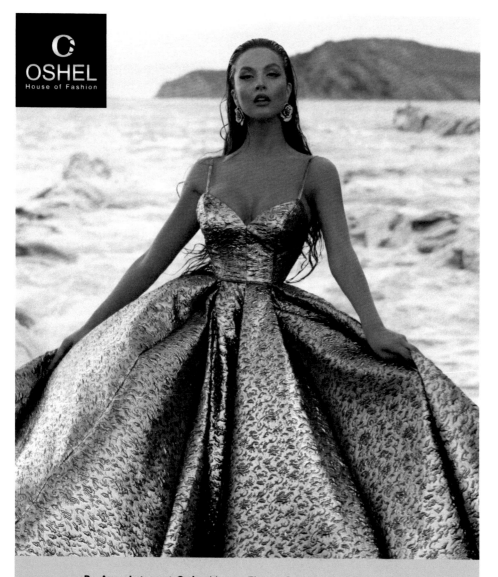

By Appointment Only: Mon to Thurs · **Open to Public:** Fri & Sat
20 Craighurst Avenue, Toronto, ON M4R 1J8 · 647.300.1047 · www.oshel.ca

Mention promo code **"VIVA"**
and receive 10% Off
your in-store purchase.

DERMEDIX COSMETIC
CLINIC

SERVICES

- Microneedling
- Vampire Facials - PRP
- Laser Hair Removal
- Photofacials / Photo Rejuvenation
- Facial Sculpting
- Body Contouring
- Skin Tightening
- Peels & Microdermabrasion

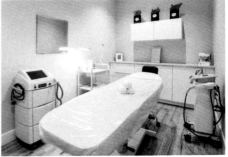

RETAIL

- Vivier Pharma skincare
- Elta MD Sunscreen
- James Read Organic Sugar Self Tanning
- Jane Irdale Organic Makeup

VIAN SHAREF

Director and founder of Dermedix, Vian Sharef has been a reputable medical esthetician and a business consultant in the beauty industry for over ten years. With honors in her medical esthetics schooling and attending York University for business & entrepreneurship. Her background in psychology, finance and banking has enriched Vian with the perfect combination of trustworthy, knowledgeable and professionalism in her field. Dermedix has all the latest medical esthetic services and has a spotless reputation for happy clients to be the platform for all women's beauty and wellness needs.

Her passion and drive is what makes Vian so well fitted for the beauty industry. "It gives me the opportunity to enhance woman's lives one woman at a time making her not only look good from the outside but feel great on the inside."

Vian has media appearances with Rogers daytime beauty show on a monthly basis and is a public motivational speaker. She gives advice to women on not only looking their best but how to strive forward feeling their best instilling a positive influence to every woman she encounters.

1416 Centre St, Unit 17, Thornhill,ON
We are located in the heart of Thornhill, Ontario,
just north of Steeles and east of Dufferin.

Tel: 905.597.2223
info@dermedix.ca

Mention promo code **"VIVA"**
and receive a complimentary
Skin Tightening Treatment.

Valued at $250.00

LIVING YOUR BEST LIFE

TOTAL RESET RETREAT

The Total Reset Retreat is a divine mind, body and soul experience. This is your opportunity to rediscover your focus and get back on track with your fitness. This amazing retreat is dedicated to you and your rejuvenation and enlightenment. You will have the opportunity to reset and reconnect with your inner self.

CHOOSE YOU!

WHY NOT YOU? WHY NOT NOW?

You've told yourself later, tomorrow, after this and after that, but when will it be your time to shine? When the business is successful? When the kids are grown up? When the to-do list gets done? You've got to decide to put YOU first above all else for everything else to succeed in your life. You deserve to live your best life NOW.

Join a community of high-vibe divine women who are on this restorative health journey together and choosing to live their best life.

PARADISE IS CLOSER THEN YOU THINK

Join us for one of your most memorable stays in the beautiful island of Aruba. This is more than just a retreat; it's your opportunity to rediscover yourself amongst the white sandy beaches of paradise. Here's what you can expect from this luxurious trip:

· Seven days of sunshine in the Caribbean
· Private luxury accommodation with breath-taking views
· Private chef to make you breakfast every morning
· Yoga, meditation and fitness to revitalize you
· Personal one-on-one coaching by Aviva
· Tranquil surroundings to bring you peace and tranquillity

Mention promo code **"VIVA"**
and receive a complimentary
Surprise Travel Gift.

ELITE LIFESTYLE & INTRODUCTIONS FIRM

Choose The Love You Deserve. For The Life You Want.

We hold a 92% match success rate

Be Selectively Efficient In Your Love Life!

Perfect Fit is Canada's leading luxury introduction firm with a strong focus on self-improvement. Our service was created for people like you who tasted success but found it an empty experience without the right person to share it with.

Our Process: We are committed to making your love life a priority. Perfect Fit is a sophisticated firm with a long standing success rate. Our business is built on integrity and the honesty we share with our clients. We have an extensive database reaching many North American and International partners. We exclusively work with a discerning successful clientele who choose to be efficient in meeting only prequalified compatible matches.

905-597-2433 | www.perfect-fit.ca
Apply with us at perfect-fit.ca/matchmaking-form

Mention promo code **"VIVA"**
and receive 20% Off your
Introduction Package of Choice.

RICHARD EMMANUEL STUDIOS
Cover photographer for
"Becoming The Total Package."

Modern Photography Studio

Richard Emmanuel has been in the family
business of photography for over 20 years.
Working alongside his father, he has
developed a unique style of photography
that is sought after from Brides to be to the
Royal Family. Over the years Richard has
founded the Richard Emmanuel Studios and
Digital Mirror which caters to client's unique
personality...from the pure organic to the
ultra modern chic.

Wedding Photography

Richard and his talented team can offer all
components of photography, videography
and Photo Booths, capturing your story
visually and bringing it to life both for social
and corporate events.

Fashionable Wedding Photographer for
both local and destination weddings.

Photography Travel Workshops. Explore
and allow photography to open the creative
tap within while travelling amongst the most
beautiful destinations in the world.

Photo Workshops

Corporate Events/Brand Activations
Exclusive services only available at the
Digital Mirror Brand provides extensive
experience for corporate events, working
with the Royal family, Government and top
brands. Providing high-quality images,
Photo Booth rentals, marketing activations
and AI photographers.
Visit www.DigitalMirror.ca for more info.

Mention Promo Code:
"VIVA" and receive an additional hour
on your Photo Booth booking.

Photo Booth Rentals

RICHARD EMMANUEL STUDIOS
PHOTOGRAPHY VIDEO PHOTO BOOTH

www.RichardEmmanuel.com
416.450.0450

LIVE YOUR DREAM
• Home Purchase • Home Sales-Staging • Interior Design

Nader Zand brings over 20 years of experience in real estate, with excellent customer service and commitment to his clients and their best interests. His integrity and follow through along with a kind spirit is what sets him apart from other industry professionals, and this is why all his clients know him as a person they can finally trust when it comes to important decisions they make about their real estate investments. Nader Zand offers The Total Package in his strategic process, so you don't have to worry about anything during this life-changing process.

 Realty Inc. Brokerage | Home of the Top Producers

Nader Zand, Sales Representative
Direct: 416.725.6061 I nader_zand@yahoo.com
Office: 416.222.8600 I Fax: 416.494.0016
183 Willowdale Ave, North York, ON M2N 4YG

MAXI

Maxi Boutique celebrates 51 years of styling women. Featuring Canadian, American and International collections.

27 Bellair Street
Toronto, Ontario

(416)-960-6294
maxibtq@gmail.com

maxibtq

Mention promo code: VIVA for 10% off
regular priced merchandise

Du Luxe

Fleur Du Luxe Canada and sister company Growers Flower Market, both have been established with over 15 years of experience servicing Toronto's most exclusive clients such as Four Seasons, Windsor Arms, Intercontinental Toronto Yorkville, Shangri-la, Ritz Carlton, and Bisha to name a few.

GFM also specializes in private and corporate events such as weddings and small landscaping projects. Our mission is to showcase beautiful long lasting creations for any special occasion.

GROWERS FLOWER MARKET
126 Avenue Rd.
Toronto, ON M5R 2H6
416-920-2442
growersflowermarket@gmail.com

NEW BLOOMING HILL FLOWERS
6241 Bathurst St.
Toronto, ON M2R 2A5
416-222-8333
newbloominghill@gmail.com

www.fleurduluxe.ca

Mention promo code **"VIVA"**
and receive 20% Off
your order.